Back Up On Skis:

My Journey Back to Ski Racing

Back Up On Skis:

My Journey Back to Ski Racing

The true story of Aubrie Mindock

AUBRIE MINDOCK

iUniverse, Inc.
Bloomington

Back Up On Skis: My Journey Back to Ski Racing
The true story of Aubrie Mindock

iUniverse books may be ordered through booksellers or by contacting:

iUniverse
1663 Liberty Drive
Bloomington, IN 47403
www.iuniverse.com
1-800-Authors (1-800-288-4677)

ISBN: 978-1-4620-5629-3 (sc)
ISBN: 978-1-4620-5630-9 (hc)
ISBN: 978-1-4620-5631-6 (ebk)

Printed in the United States of America

iUniverse rev. date: 12/28/2011

Back up on Skis

The true story of Aubrie Mindock and her journey back on skis after two accidents that almost killed her and took away the sport she loves most

Acknowledgements

I would like to thank my family for the support and love they have shown me. I am grateful for having such a wonderful, loving family. God has really blessed me and given me so much. He has made me strong and I want to acknowledge God for everything he has done for me and for all of the special blessings he has given me and my family.

I would like to dedicate this book to Nana and Papa Reis. I know that I do not get to see you guys a lot and I wish that I could see you more often. I just want to let you know that I love you guys and miss you. Hopefully in the future I can visit you and spend more time with you.

Contents

Foreword

My family has always been very supportive of me. They are the reason that I am able to write this book as well as the others that I have published. Growing up my parents always told me, "Go for your dreams." They have taught me that in order to succeed in life I must work hard and do what I love.

I never thought that I would be an author. Writing has been something that I enjoy but I never thought that I would be an author. When I was 17 years old I wrote my first book, "A New Beginning: Fighting to get back up on Skis," but I never thought that it would actually get published and that I would even have more books coming out.

My family has had a huge influence on my writing as well as in my life. They are the reason why I decided to tell you my story. My parents believe that by writing books somehow I can help others. My goal is to have an influence on someone else and show them that their dreams are not impossible. Through writing I want to show people that life is a gift and must be lived well. It does not matter where you come from, you can always succeed and be something great.

As many of you already know when I was 15 I was in a bad ski accident that almost took away my life and my skiing. I had to fight and work real hard to get back up on skis. It was not an easy thing to do and I almost did not succeed. Through hard work I was able to not only race again but make it to a college ski team. I was thrilled and so stoked that my hard work paid off.

What many of you do not know is that during my second race of my freshman year of college I had another bad fall. I was on my way to Nationals before I crashed and almost died a second time. After my fall I remember going to Heaven where I saw my grandfather who had died several months before. While the paramedics were working on my body that was lifeless on the snow I was in Heaven, where everything was peaceful and calm.

When I came back to Earth I found myself lost and confused, like I was when I was 15, after my first accident. I had no clue as to why another bad accident happened and I basically knew that I had to start all over with racing and training. Once again it was going to be a long, rough road back to the slopes but I knew that I would be able to make it.

I did make it back to skis. Against all odds I even made it to Nationals where my team and I placed 5th. Today I am teaching skiing as well as once again going for the Olympics. This will be my last attempt at the Olympics because I want to move on to some other great adventures. I do not know where my life will take me but I do know that whatever adventure I have it will be amazing. Through all of this hardship and fighting to get back up to the sport I love I learned that perseverance and having difficult situations only makes you stronger. In order to grow and be a strong person you must have some adversity.

Sometimes I find myself wondering why bad things have to happen not only to me but to others. It is often confusing as to why we must go through so much pain. Of course you do not ask for bad things to happen to you but they just do, and it is difficult at times to deal with it. When something bad happens to me I find strength through God. What does God want me to do with this bad stuff? How does he want me to handle it? Why was I put through this? These are some of the questions we might ask ourselves when an unplanned event happens. The thing is we do not know why bad things happen but God has a plan, and he will use the bad and turn it into good.

When reading my story think about how some of the negative things in your life can be turned into good. What is God doing to make your life better? How is he using you? Sometimes we get caught up in the "Why me?" way of thinking but try hard to really think about what good can come out of whatever your situation may be. Think about how you can turn your negative into a positive and really make a difference in this world.

15 years old: The accident

I was going fast. I do not know how fast but it was fast. My brother Austin was close behind me and I was beating him as we raced down the mountain. It was getting late in the day and the light was flat, making it difficult to see what was ahead of me. The snow and the sky looked as though it was one. When the light is flat it makes it more dangerous for a skier or boarder and that is why most people call it a day at the first signs of flat light.

All of the sudden it happened. I caught the edge of my ski in a rut and went flying in the air. As I came down my knee landed on the binding of my ski, causing damage and my ski pole stabbed me in the ribs, causing them to break. I felt a crack in my rib cage and immediately stopped breathing. I kept tumbling head over heels down the mountain until I finally came to a stop.

Confused and dazed I laid on the snow, gasping for air but nothing filled my lungs. I saw a stream of blood land on the white snow and at first I thought that I was bleeding from my lip. I thought that I had bit my lip or tongue during the fall but soon came to realize that I was bleeding from my lung. Something was terribly wrong and I had the feeling that I was going to die.

There was no pain, none at all. As I slowly rolled to my knees I could feel a crunching feeling but nothing hurt. I remember looking down at the chair lift, where my brother was standing. Desperately I tried to yell down to him, but I couldn't. When you cannot breathe you cannot talk. Somehow I needed to find a way to tell Austin that I was okay and not in pain. He was watching me die from below and was helpless. I did not want him to think that I was in pain so I did whatever I could to let him know that I would be fine.

A few seconds later I thought, "How will my family deal with the loss of me?" My mother lost her first husband to a drunk driver, and my father, he couldn't lose his ski buddy. "How will my brother cope with watching me die?" He was going to witness the death of his sister, how scary for him. Soon, a feeling of warmth came over me. It felt like someone was wrapping a warm blanket around me. "Okay God, I'm ready," I thought to myself as I felt my body weaken. I was fading away.

All of the sudden I thought, "No, I can't die. My mother needs me. I can't leave my family." At the thought of that I took my first breath of air in about a minute, maybe over. It felt so good to breathe again but I was not out of the woods, not even close. I was in serious trouble and somehow I had to find a way to survive.

A man had brought my skis down and handed them to me. "Are you okay?" he asked, concerned about the blood he saw on the snow. I didn't reply except "Thanks for my skis." He followed me down the rest of the way to make sure I would make it. Because of my knee being damaged I was forced to ski on one ski, which was difficult. Luckily my right knee was injured because I am pretty good with one ski if the ski is on my left foot.

When I got to the chair I saw my brother waiting for me. I was a little upset and scared and so was he. I could see the look on Austin's face, the look of "My sister is hurt bad." I just told him that we should get on the chair and get to the top of the mountain. I was going to try to ski home and get to my dad instead of go to ski patrol (mountain paramedics) because I really did not want the medical attention.

The ride up the chair was awful. I kept coughing up blood and I thought that I was going to stop breathing again. All I could think about was getting to the top of the mountain and getting off the lift. If you have never been on a chair lift there is a safety bar that comes down. Most people do not use the bar because experienced skiers think it is silly. Well, in my circumstance we defiantly put the bar down, just in case I passed out. I was so scared and was just thinking, "Just get off the chair. Just make it to the top. Please God, let me make it to the top."

After what seemed like forever I reached the top of the mountain. Getting off the chair lift felt good, but soon I came to realize that I had a slow, agonizing ride down to safety. There was no way that I could ski with one ski all the way home. I was still coughing up blood and realized that I needed help and fast. Now, I could have laid down on the snow and waited for help to come to me but sometimes ski patrol takes a while and I needed help immediately so I decided to ski to them.

The Vista Haus warming hut was just a couple seconds from where I was standing so I said to Austin, "I am going to ski to patrol. I need to get help." Austin assisted me to the Vista Haus and helped me gather my skis and put my gear away. As I was walking inside I could feel a "crunch, crunch" in my knee but it didn't hurt. It just felt a little weird, like something wasn't right. It kind of felt like there was a sponge inside my knee.

I remember being scared and not wanting to get help but I knew that I needed it. In the past the ski patrol and I never got along so I was afraid of them. When I am not hurt I am typically the last person off the mountain and the ski patrol is constantly yelling at me to slow down. I even had my pass pulled a few times for going too fast in the slow zone, so I was afraid that I was going to get yelled at again by the patrol.

Instead of going inside their office and asking for help I decided to sit at a table and wait for a patroller to come out. Even though I was severely injured I was still avoiding patrol due to being afraid. Growing up I had been healthy and never really had anything serious happen so when I started coughing up blood and saw that my knee was crushed I was terrified and part of avoiding help was because I didn't know what to expect. I didn't know what was going to happen to me.

Well, it did not take long for a patroller to come out of the office. I remember seeing her walk out and past me. It was now or never so I decided to grab her attention. "I need help," I said to her as she passed by. She didn't hesitate to help me. "I don't know what

I did. I am coughing up blood and I stopped breathing. My knee looks funny too," I told her as she kneeled down to get eye level to me. She told me to hold on and she had to leave me for a minute to grab some people to help out. When she walked off a feeling of relief came upon me. I was finally going to be saved.

Less than a minute later it seemed that the entire patrol were around me. One man got eye level to me and told me what to expect. He could tell that I was scared. "How old are you?" the man asked. "15." I replied. "We are going to take good care of you. You are going to be alright," the man reassured me as he put an oxygen mask over my mouth. Since there were so many people around me I started to panic a little. I started to realize how serious my injuries were and that I actually should have been dead before I even had a chance to make it up the mountain. "Aubrie, hold my hand until we have to go," the man said as he reached his hand out.

"Let's get her in the sled. We have to go," another patroller said as he finished taking my blood pressure. My blood pressure was dropping and they had to move fast to get me off the mountain. I was carried outside and put in the toboggan (medical sled). Once in the sled I started to cry. I think I was crying because I was scared, but this worried the ski patrol who thought that I was in a lot of pain, which I wasn't. "I want my dad," I said to a young man who was kneeling next to me. He told me that they will get a hold of my dad and I will be able to see him at the hospital. Then he went on to ask if I was in any pain. "No," I replied as I started to doze off.

"She's starting to fade. We have to go," the man yelled out to everyone around him. "Stay awake for me Aubrie. We are going to get you to the hospital," He said as a female patroller grabbed the handle bars of the sled. As we started to take off the female at the head of the sled said, "Aubrie, if you need anything just let us know and we will stop. Just try and stay awake for us." I didn't say anything and just kept my eyes focused on the sky. Breathing started to get difficult again and I started to spit up more blood. "Please God, let me live," I thought as I felt myself fade into a sleep once again.

There was a man on a snowmobile who followed close behind me. He could tell that something was wrong so he yelled, "Stop!" I remember stopping and seeing a blur of red coats around me. "Aubrie, open your eyes. Come on. Stay with us. We are almost there," The man and woman said as they desperately tried to keep me focused on survival. "There is blood in her mask. Clean it out and call for assistance," The man said to the woman. I remember feeling them tug at my clothing a little and adjust my oxygen. "Come on Aubrie, open your eyes," They said again. "Stay with us," and then everything went black.

When I woke up I was at the bottom of the mountain. My boots were off and so was my coat. I was basically stripped down to my favorite U.S. Ski Team t-shirt. It felt good to have all of the heavy clothing off and those uncomfortable, plastic boots removed. As I looked around the room I noticed 3 patrollers, one of which was on the phone with the hospital. "We have a 15 year old female, trauma," he said to whoever it was on the other line.

Someone noticed that I was waking up and soon several people were around me. "Aubrie, you are at the base of the mountain. We have an ambulance coming for you," It was the female who had the handlebars of my sled. She was real nice and reassured me that I was going to make it. "Where is my dad?" I asked as I looked at her with teary eyes. She told me that my dad was in the medical center because he had broken his finger skiing earlier. I never skied with my dad that day. He came out later and took a fall. I smiled a little because it was kind of funny that both my dad and I got hurt on the same day.

I was very tired and all I could think about was sleep. The ski patrol however, did not allow me to sleep. "You need to stay awake, Aubrie. Just keep talking to us. The ambulance will be here soon." I remember hearing the sirens which were loud and shrill. Once again fear struck me. I had never been in an ambulance before and I didn't want a bunch of people around me, touching me. Having a bunch of strange men around me scared me but I knew that I had to go with them. The ski patrol knew that I was scared so they held my hand until help arrived.

The paramedics rushed towards me and they had a lot of equipment with them. I remember seeing a backboard, a stretcher and something on the stretcher which I now know was a heart monitor. They also had a big black bag with a lot of medical supplies in it. One of the men grabbed my head and asked the patrol, "Did she hit her head? Does she have any spinal injuries? Why didn't you c-spine her?" The other man got eye level to me, like the patrollers on the top of the mountain did. "What is your name?" He asked as he put a blood pressure cuff on my right arm. "Aubrie, Aubrie Mindock," I responded.

My eyes started to fill with tears and I got scared and pulled away a little from the men. "It's okay. We aren't going to hurt you," The man at my head said. He started to tell me everything that was going to happen and asked me if I had hit my head or hurt my neck or back. I told him that my back didn't hurt and that I wanted my dad. "Has anyone contacted her parents?" The man asked the patrollers. "Yes, her father is at the hospital," One of the patrollers responded. The man looked back at me and said, "Aubrie, your dad is already at the hospital. He will be waiting for you there." Knowing that my dad was already at the ER calmed me.

The man holding my head kept talking to me in a calm voice. "Do you have any pain? Do you have any allergies to medications? Can you tell me what happened?" It was a little difficult to talk because I was having problems breathing. The paramedic was patient and didn't try to force answers out of me. Instead he turned to the ski patrol. "Did anyone witness the accident?" He asked the patrollers. One of the patrollers told the paramedic that my brother had witnessed it but he skied home after I got to safety. The paramedic looked at me again and said, "We are going to take good care of you. We are going to make you as comfortable as possible. Let us know if you start having a lot of pain."

I started to get thirsty and asked the paramedics for water. "You have to have an empty stomach because you might need surgery," The man at my head said. This concerned the men because they started to think that I was going into shock. "Aubrie, we need you to keep talking to us. Are you dizzy? Do you feel sleepy? Are you cold?"

The men asked. I didn't really respond because I was trying to stay focused on what was going on around me.

The man who took my blood pressure looked concerned. "It is really low. We have to go now," he said to his partner. "Aubrie, we are going to put you on the stretcher now and take you to the hospital," the man at my head said to me. They carefully lifted me up, put me on a stretcher and put a blanket on me. "It is going to be a little cold outside but once we get in the ambulance we will put the heat on for you," one of the men said as I was being wheeled out. Once outside I didn't mind the cold air. It actually felt good but then again I love the snow and cold.

A police officer was also on the scene. Since I was underage I think there had to be an officer. As I was being wheeled out to the ambulance I remember feeling some pain from the bumps on the road. The ground was icy and snowpack, making it a little difficult for the medics to get through it. "Here, hold my hand," the officer said to me as tears filled my eyes. "It hurts and I want my dad," I said back to him. "Your dad is at the hospital waiting for you. Squeeze my hand and keep talking to me," He said back to me. I took his hand and held on to it until the medics got me in the ambulance. "Hang in there kiddo. You'll be alright," the officer said as the doors of the ambulance closed.

"Are we going emergent?" The medic in the back asked the driver. "Yes," the driver said as he flipped on the lights and sirens. The ride down the mountain was very long and slow. The driver could not go that fast because it was icy. Since it had snowed the night before, there was a fresh sheet of ice on the road, making driving difficult. The flat light didn't help making black ice visible either.

"We are going to get you there as fast as we can. Just keep talking to me," The man in the back said as he hooked me up to an IV and a blood pressure cuff. I was getting sleepy again and I remember the medic kept telling me to keep my eyes open and stay with him. "Keep talking to me. Keep your eyes open for me." I tried to listen to him but I couldn't. I was just too tired and I passed out again.

I remember waking up to the sight of blood on my oxygen mask. The paramedic took the mask off and leaned me over to my left side. "It's okay, just cough." When I was done getting sick he put me on my back and said, "I have to lift your shirt up a little and check your abdomen and ribs. You could have some internal bleeding." As he was poking around in my rib cage I winced. He noticed and said, "I think you have some broken ribs and they may have scraped your lung a little." When he said that I got scared but he told me that the doctors would make me better and that I was going to be alright.

To keep me from passing out again the paramedic started to ask me about what I want to be when I grow up. I told him, "An Olympic skier." We talked a little about my ski racing and the other sports that I like to play and he said, "If you want to be an Olympic skier then you can. You can be whatever you want to be." He kept asking me how I was feeling and every time I would spit up blood he would change my oxygen mask and clean up the blood around me. He would also have to take my blood pressure after every episode of blood spitting so I tried my hardest to not get sick. I didn't like how the cuff felt on my arm. It was tight and pinched.

After what seemed like forever I was finally at the hospital. The driver stopped the ambulance and came around back to open the doors. Both of the medics wheeled me in the hospital where my dad was waiting. As my dad walked up I smiled. "Sir, are you her father?" Someone asked him. "Yes, I am." Finally I got to see my dad and I was no longer alone.

The hospital wasn't much better than the ambulance. I had to go through a lot more tests. The only thing that was good about it was that my dad was with me. There was a moment when the doctors left my dad and I alone in the room. My dad and I actually did not talk about what had happened to me. Instead we joked that both of us got hurt on the same day, which was pretty funny. I was glad that my dad was with me and when I saw his finger cast I had a little smile. "I'm going to have a leg cast and you have a finger cast," I said to him. We both laughed a little. "Wait until mom finds out about this," my dad said in response to my comment. We both smiled a bit.

I had a torn ACL, LCL, meniscus, fractured knee, broken ribs and a bruised lung. My lung was bruised to the point where it was bleeding and that is why I was coughing up blood. I didn't have to stay in the hospital overnight because the doctors were able to stabilize me and I was stable long enough to go home. I remember that I was in the hospital for what seemed like hours though. I think it was hours. It was forever.

When I got home my brother was waiting for us. He didn't know that my dad had also gotten hurt that morning and when he found out he made a joke out of it. "Good thing mom isn't here because I don't think that she would be joking with us," we all said as we laughed a little. I couldn't really laugh too hard because it hurt too bad, and I was also exhausted and not feeling well. My dad ended up cooking a little dinner for my brother and I but I didn't really eat. Instead I went straight to bed. I had a long recovery ahead and I didn't know if I would ever be able to race again or make it to the Olympics.

Challenging days ahead

I did need surgery on my knee. About a month after the accident I remember my parents taking me to Swedish Medical Center for surgery. I remember the cold room that I was put in and the smell of latex. My mother was sitting to my left and she was holding my hand. "Aubrie, this will be over with soon. You will be back up on the slopes before you know it," She said in a reassuring voice.

I remember shivering uncontrollably. The nurses kept bringing me warm blankets but they did not help. When one blanket would cool off they would immediately have another one to warm me up. My arms turned white with goose bumps and for some reason I just would not warm up. It was not fun being back in the hospital, knowing that I would have to go through even more.

"Aubrie, since you broke your ribs and injured your lung we are going to have to put a tube down your throat to help you breathe during surgery," The doctor said as he walked in the room. "You will not feel a thing and it will just be in for a little while," He said. The thought of having a tube in my throat scared me and I tried not to think about it.

The nurse walked in next. "Aubrie, I am going to put your IV in. You are going to feel a little pinch," She said as she tied a purple thing around my left arm. Finding a vein to put the IV in was difficult because I was so cold. I remember she rubbed my arm a little and poked at the veins with her fingers, trying to find a good one. "I know this hurts," She said as she fumbled with the IV.

After the IV was in my mother was allowed to give me her sweater. I could only put my right arm through because my left arm had the IV. Her sweater was nice and warm and I didn't want to take it off but when they wheeled me into the OR I had to give my mother's sweatshirt back. Giving it back to her was difficult because having something of hers was comforting and I felt safe holding my mother's sweater.

I remember feeling really tired because they had put the stuff to make me go to sleep in my body. When I got to the OR I was helped on a cold metal table. It seemed that everything in the room was spinning. The lights were blurry and seemed to blend into one big light. As I laid down I struggled to keep my eyes open and stay awake. In the ambulance I was told to stay awake so it was just natural for me to fight the need to close my eyes. Eventually sleep overwhelmed me and I closed my eyes.

When I woke up the doctor told me that I needed to hold still because he had to take the tube out of my throat. He did it real quick and it was for the most part painless. I remember seeing my mother who had some soda and crackers for me but I didn't feel like eating anything. I just was not hungry. "Aubrie, the doctor said that everything went well and you can go home tonight," my mother said after I refused the crackers. I was thrilled that I didn't have to spend the night in the hospital and that I was going to get to sleep in my own bed.

The ride home from Swedish was fun. My mother played my favorite music and I got plenty of calls from my family. I was so glad that my mother's parents called. I really enjoy talking to them and unfortunately I do not get to see them much. "Mom, when can I ski again?" I asked in between phone calls. "I don't know Aubrie. You have to see how you heal up," She said as she pulled in the garage of my home. I really wanted to get back up on skis and just could not wait any longer. I had to ski but couldn't.

It would be a long summer of pain and fighting to get back on skis. Getting back to the mountain was not an easy task. I spent many hours in the gym and at physical therapy. No one knew if I would even be able to race again and making the Olympic team was important to me. I wanted that more than anything but my dream of ever being a ski racer again was basically gone.

It was now Thanksgiving Day and my dad said, "Aubrie, I'd like to see you race again. I think you can do it." He was right and immediately I was back on the course, plowing through the gates like they were not even there. Getting back up was awesome and the only thing that I wanted. Through hard work and determination I was not only able to get back up on the race course, I also skied my way to college.

After the accident I learned that hard work gets a person where they want to be in life. In order to succeed you must overcome your obstacles and pick yourself back up. If you chose to stay down and not even try then you will never know where you could have gone. In order to succeed you must fail first and learn, then you can have your dreams come true.

Your turn: Write about an experience in your life that was challenging. What happened to you? How did you overcome it?

_____
_____
_____
_____
_____
_____
_____
_____
_____
_____
_____
_____
_____
_____
_____
_____
_____
_____
_____
_____
_____
_____
_____
_____
_____
_____
_____
_____
_____
_____
_____
_____

Your turn: Write about a time when you picked yourself up after a bad incident happened. How did you feel when you succeeded? What is success to you?

Your Turn: When I was in the back of the ambulance the paramedic tried to keep me awake by talking about what I want to be when I grow up. I said, "An Olympic skier." What do you want to be when you grow up?

_____

_____

_____

_____

_____

_____

_____

_____

_____

_____

_____

_____

_____

_____

_____

_____

_____

_____

_____

_____

_____

_____

_____

_____

_____

_____

_____

_____

_____

_____

_____

Your Turn: I have a strong belief in God. God has really helped me get through some tough times in my life. When I was on the snow not breathing I prayed for my mom, dad and brother. I prayed that they would be alright after I died. What are your religious beliefs? What does your family believe?

Your turn: What do you enjoy doing with your free time? Maybe you play sports or are in the band. What makes you happy?

College Ski Team

I worked extremely hard in high school to perfect my skiing and racing ability. After my accident my goals were to not only get on a college ski team but also make the Olympics. When the time came for me to go to college I had several choices of schools to decide from. I had been accepted in all of the schools that I applied to but I really wanted to either go to Western State College or Fort Lewis College because of the ski areas that surrounded those schools.

I chose to go to Fort Lewis College in Durango, CO because there was literally a ski area on the campus. Not only that but areas such as Purgatory, Wolf Creek, and Telluride are less than 2 hours away. What a perfect place to go to college. Being able to ski every day and be in the beautiful mountains was something that I have always wanted to do growing up. Although I skied in Breckenridge as a kid I went to school in Denver. I had always wanted to live in a mountain town and be able to hike, bike, rock climb and most of all ski.

What a blast college was. My teammates were so much fun and the campus was just beautiful. With many hiking and running trails I was able to stay plenty busy and keep up a good workout routine. Immediately I got involved in two Christian groups and athletics. I had the life and it seemed that everything was going to work out and that all of my issues from my accident at 15 were in the past and over.

One night my friends and I decided to go night tubing in a river that is in town. It was the middle of November and yes, it was snowing. Being the crazy college students that we were we decided that it would be fun to put on our bikini's and swim shorts and ride down the rapids on little tubes that were not much bigger than us.

"Aubrie, come on. This will be the adventure of a lifetime. The rapids are still big and the river is fast. Let's do this!" One of my friends blurted out as she jumped in the icy river. I didn't even have a chance to put half my body in the cold river before I started to shiver uncontrollably. "This is freezing," I said to no one in particular as I jumped on my tube and started to paddle out to the rapids. "We must be nuts," I thought to myself.

I only spent about 20 minutes in the frigid water before I was too cold to tube any longer. As I approached a rapid I noticed the river bank became shallow and I paddled towards the shallower water before jumping off my tube and walking out of the river. "I can't take it anymore. It is too cold," I said to my friends as they paddled towards the rapid. Another friend came with me. "I agree Aubrie. I'm freezing too," She said as we walked towards my car. My other friends decided to stay in the river longer before getting out but they too eventually got too cold and were forced to warm up.

After our little tubing adventure we all went to one of my friends place and sat around the fire and drank warm drinks. We joked about how cold we got and how that was a once in a lifetime adventure. Since it was the night before Thanksgiving break we decided to have a slumber party and just make the most out of our last night for a week in Durango.

Not only were my new friends a blast, the team was a blast too. I went to Fort Lewis College to ski, not just to hang out and have fun with everyone. Since I was going to try out for the Olympics I had work to do. Being on a college ski team is tough work, both physically and academically. In order to compete and even train with the team you are required to have at least a 3.0 GPA. That means you have to have all A's and B's. School was challenging because I had to miss a lot to train, which meant when everyone else was going out to parties and having a fun weekend I was stuck inside studying and playing catch up.

Colleges are known for their wild parties and crazy nights but I never had a night like that. I was not able to go out, get drunk and party away like a lot of the students. Since I was a college athlete my schedule consisted of school, studying and skiing. Several times a week I was able to find a couple hours to get away with my Christian friends, which was a good break from all of the skiing and studying. However, I was not able to spend as much time as I would have liked to spend with them because of my busy schedule.

Sometimes being so busy and having to stay sober so I could perform and stay healthy on the mountain was tough. There were times when I just wanted to go out and experience what many of the other students were doing but I couldn't. I would often hear people talk about how they do not remember their nights or they would come up with funny stories about how their weekend was or how much fun that party was the other night. There were times when I just wanted to experience that for myself. All I wanted was one night where I could just do what most of the other students were doing but I couldn't. I had to stay focused on school and skiing.

Because I was staying focused on school and skiing I started to really do well in my events and I actually was on my way to Nationals. My parents were so supportive and excited that I was not only back up on the race course but also that all of my hard work prevailed and that I was really a serious competitor. Most of all they were proud that because of skiing and my motivation to stay on the team and compete my grades were good and I almost had a 4.0 GPA my first semester of college. I was thriving and living the life. My future as a professional athlete was looking bright again and it seemed as though noting could stop me.

Death comes to my door:
My second near fatal accident

It was my second race of the ski season of my freshman year of college. The day was cold and snowy, like it usually is on race day. I was a little run down with a head cold and I just wanted the day to be over with. My mother was at the start with me, waiting for my number to be called. She was going to stay with me until I was called to get into line and wait for my run. "Mom, I'm going to just go for it. I really want to do well and make it to Nationals," I said minutes before I was supposed to go. "Go for it Aubrie. You'll do great. You are already on your way to Nationals."

I had only two races to go until Nationals and already things were looking good for me and my team. My team and I were already in first place and I just really wanted to give it a go. I knew what I was doing and I was not afraid of speed. I love going fast and speeding down the mountain, and in a race course I can go as fast as I want without being yelled at by patrol.

Since I was sick my mom was helping me stay warm by giving me warm water and she even gave me her coat until I was supposed to go. Ski racers have to wear tight clothes called speed suits. These suits are very thin and do not keep you warm at all. My dad had taken my warm coat and my ski pants to the finish, where he would give them back to me after my run.

"Aubrie, you are in first place right now. You have it girl. Just do your best and when you are done your dad and I will take you to get a good meal," My mom said as she hugged me. She could tell that I was tired and not feeling well so she tried to motivate me to tough it out. I smiled at my mom's words and we started to talk about the warm fire place but all I could think about was just getting done with my last run and doing well. I knew that my dad was waiting for me at the finish and I just wanted to get down the mountain so I could get my coat on and get ready for awards.

Finally my section was called to get ready to race. I remember looking at my mom and said, "Well, here I go. It's almost my turn." My mom said, "Okay Aubrie, do your best." There was a girl in front of me. She was my opponent. She turned around and we started talking a little. Before she went for her run I said to her, "Good luck. Have fun." She said back, "Thank you, same to you." A few seconds after she left the start I was ready to go. I gave my mother a quick hug goodbye and she said, "See you at the finish. Have fun out there," then we parted, and I headed to the start. "Beep, Beep, Beep," I heard the gate's clock count down. Before I knew it I was off and on my way.

The course was beautiful and set up perfect. I was flying and actually doing real well until the binding of my ski came loose and popped off. I do not remember much about the accident but I do remember hearing people scream as I went down. When I woke up I noticed that my red helmet flew off my head, which shouldn't have happened because it was on tight. My goggles were broken and so was my right arm. My boots were unbuckled and I couldn't move my right knee.

"Aubrie, Aubrie, can you hear me? Stay with us. You had a bad accident and we think you may have a broken neck and a fractured skull. Do not move your head," I heard my coach frantically say. I was dazed and confused and did not know what happened. "She has blood coming out of her ears," I heard someone say. "Get the ski patrol down here now," someone else yelled out. "Aubrie can you hear me? Stay with us. Help is coming," someone said to me as I went unconscious.

I started to fade in and out and I only caught glimpses of what was going on around me. I remember seeing two ski patrollers jump from the chair lift, which was almost above me. "We have to get her down the mountain now," one of the men said. The other man started to unzip my speed suit and he started to check for other injuries. "You need to talk to us. Stay awake. Do not go to sleep," They kept telling me. "Hey, talk to me. Stay with me," they kept saying over and over. I actually didn't listen to them because I did not understand what they were saying. I was so dizzy and sick that I could not focus. All I could focus on was sleep. Concentrating on what the rescuers were telling me to do was impossible.

Immediately I heard over someone's radio, "Cancel the race. We need to stop the race. There is a serious injury," I heard my number being called out as well. "Number 83 is down. She will not get a score." When I heard that I broke down in tears. I had never fallen during a race and I didn't want to hear that over the radio. Hearing that I was possibly not going to qualify for nationals was horrible and I did not want to give up. I wanted to finish the race but I couldn't, not with a possible fractured neck.

"Aubrie it is real important that you do not move. You have a possible fractured neck and your skull is fractured. You need to try and stay awake," A ski patroller said. I did my best to stay awake and fight to stay alive but it didn't work. As I slipped into a sleep again I heard someone say to me, "Aubrie talk to us. Keep talking to us. Don't give up." Someone tugged at my shirt and tried to wake me but everything went black.

I kept catching glimpses of what was going on. I remember hearing people screaming from the lift and the patrol trying to keep people calm around me. People started to panic and I remember someone saying, "If you do not know her or are not on her team then you need to back up and leave. We need room to work." People were getting anxious and agitated. "We need people to get out of here. Leave if you do not need to be here," I heard someone yell out again.

With all of the commotion going on around me I started to get upset. I remember thinking that I didn't want a huge crowd of strangers around me. I wanted people to get away from me and leave me alone. The ski patrol must have noticed that I was getting frustrated because someone got up and walked toward the crowd. "This is the last time that I am going to tell you guys to leave. Get out of here now," They yelled out again. "We need room to get her off the mountain."

With all of the yelling I became upset. "Hold my hand and talk to me. Keep fighting. We are going to do everything we can to help you and make you comfortable," A female said as I tried to see what people were doing to me. "My parents are waiting for me at the finish," I said to no one in particular. Someone responded by saying, "We know. We were able to get a hold of them." That made me more comfortable, knowing that my parents knew what happened to me.

I really do not remember much about what went on around me but I do know that I pretty much died and everyone around me was doing whatever they could to bring me back. "She's fading fast," I heard a female say to someone around her. I heard a man's voice say, "We can't lose her. No matter what do not let her go." I was fading in and out and from the sound of people's voices around me I knew that I was hurt bad.

I remember someone giving me oxygen. The person who put the oxygen on me said to the person holding my head, "Keep an eye on her airway. Make sure she doesn't stop breathing." Next someone put a brace on my arm and stabilized my leg. I remember the backboard and being strapped down. I also remember someone asking, "Are you comfortable? I know this is hard but there are things we can do to make you more comfortable." I never really responded to anyone's questions. All I could think about was staying awake and fighting passing out.

"Aubrie I know it is difficult to focus but we really need you to keep talking to us," the female patroller said as she got a blanket for me. I was so cold from the weather, laying on the snow and from being in shock. It was awful and I couldn't stop shivering. "Here, take my jacket and put it on her. Keep her warm," my coach said as he gave his coat to the ski patrol. The coat felt good but with my back on the snow I was still freezing.

The last thing I remember was hearing people around me crying. There were people on the lift who were screaming and freaking out and I could hear the panic in the voices of those who were trying to keep me alive. I remember seeing more red coats come towards me, and I heard voices on the radio asking about my condition. Before everything went black I heard my coach, "Aubrie, you are going to make it. You will be okay. Hang in there." I didn't hang in there. Shortly after my coach told me to stay with him my entire world came to an end. No one thought that I was going to come back and make it out alive.

I was still on the snow when I went to Heaven. The ski patrol had not had a chance to get me down the mountain when I left everything behind to join God. I remember everything going black then waking up in a big garden with red and pink flowers. The garden went on forever. I was in the middle of the garden but I do not know how I knew that it was the middle because the garden was so big. Standing to my left was my grandfather, Nick DeMayo, who I call PopPop. PopPop had died several months before my accident and now I was with him, once again.

PopPop and I were smiling at each other. Well he was defiantly smiling and I was just happy. I remember seeing white all around me. The light was white, and so were the clothes that PopPop and I were in. Everything was beautiful and a feeling of peace came over me. I felt safe, like nothing could hurt me and there was no more pain or suffering. What was going on with my body no longer mattered because I was not there. I was safe in God's kingdom. I was free from all of my troubles and every bad thing that happened to me on Earth was gone, like it never existed. I loved where I was and felt so happy and free.

I remember having a choice of whether or not I was going to come back to Earth. Actually, I was going to stay in Heaven but right before I had the chance to go with PopPop I heard my mother's voice, "Aubrie, Aubrie, wake up. Please don't die. Please come back." All of a sudden everything went black and I woke up in the hospital with people all around me.

There was a female ski patroller holding my right hand. Her voice was calm and gentle. "Aubrie, can you open your eyes?" I heard people talking to me but I couldn't open my eyes. They were so swollen and I was still slipping in and out. "Aubrie, can you hear me?" I heard the female ask. Slowly I was able to open just enough to make out figures in red coats and I could hear my mom's voice. As I started to get use to the lights in the room I was able to open my eyes more and more.

"Mom, where am I? What happened?" I asked as I tried to find her. I could hear my mother but I could not see her. My mom walked over to me. "You are in the hospital. You have some serious injuries," She said as she rubbed my head. I closed my eyes again and could hear my mother talking to a female about how I wanted to be in the Olympics and how I skied my way to college. She talked about my grandfather being in the 10th mountain division and how my dad was a ski instructor. It was good that my mom was talking about all of this because it kept her calm. My mom is usually calm when it comes to emergencies anyway.

"Mom, I saw PopPop," I said as I opened my eyes again. "I went to Heaven and you woke me up," I said to her. My mother believed me and cried. "How was PopPop? Is he Happy?" She asked with tears in her eyes. I told her all about the garden and the smile that PopPop had on his face. I told her that he looked like himself but younger. My mother was stunned about what I told her but she said, "Aubrie, I know that you went to Heaven. I know that this is true. I saw an angel once as well and almost went to Heaven when I was a kid." I listened to my mother's story and we smiled at each other when we both realized that God will take care of us after we die.

I didn't stay awake for long and since I do not really remember what happened I'll tell you that I did have a fractured skull. I actually went back to school after a couple days of rest and I did have seizures due to the head injury. My roommate and sweet mates were amazing and really did what they could to take care of me. They even rushed me back to the hospital after I had a seizure and waited there until I was released.

I also had a broken knee and a broken arm so I was basically in a full body cast. My neck had a small fracture and I was even put in a neck brace for a few weeks. Due to me having limited mobility my roommates and sweet mates stepped up and helped me get to class and even helped me email my professors so I could tell them what happened. When it came to typing my papers they would do the typing while I told them what I wanted to write. It is amazing how people step up for someone who is in need. If it wasn't for them I would have had to drop out of school that semester and take some time off school.

As I started to recover people on the campus wanted me to speak about overcoming obstacles. At first I was nervous because I stuttered due to my head injury. No one seemed to care though and everyone was very supportive and understanding. "Aubrie, we would like you to talk about your experience in front of our group. No one will judge you. We are a Christian group and we would like to hear about how you overcame this," A man said after he overheard my plans to get back up on skis once again. After talking to him about what I was going to say I agreed to speak.

I am so glad that I had the opportunity to talk to people about what it is like to have something bad happen to you and be able to get back up. Although I do not remember a lot of the details about my accident I was still able to encourage others to pick themselves back up after something bad happens. When I was speaking to these groups of people I still had two black eyes that were swollen, and a body cast on. The amazing thing is that people did not seem to notice that I was injured. What they did see was my determination to move on and make the most out of this bad situation.

It wasn't long before I was back on skis and racing once again. I was actually competing with one arm and a broken knee. My arm was in a full arm cast and my knee was in a huge brace but I just had to get back up. I remember everyone looking at me with these nervous looks on their faces. My parents were terrified as were my coaches. I couldn't fall, no matter what. One more fall and I would be dead for sure. It was actually probably a little dumb of me to even be on skis but I felt like I didn't have a choice. Racing is my passion and there was no way that I was not going to get back up.

Against all odds I made it to Nationals. Making Nationals was the best day of my life. I still remember that phone call when the person on the other line said, "Congratulations Aubrie. You made it to Nationals." Immediately I told my parents who were just so happy for me. I placed 5th at Nationals and then took the rest of the season to get over my injuries.

Today I am going to try to make the Olympics one more time and this will be the last time that I go for it not because I can't race anymore but because I want to move on to bigger and better things. It is amazing how life takes you in all kinds of weird directions. One day you wake up wanting to be an Olympic athlete and a professional skier and the next you want to try something else. No matter what I do with my life I know that I will be happy and that my life will be amazing.

I learned through all of my trials that I need to enjoy life because it can be taken away just like that. You never know when your time is up so you must enjoy the time that you have and make the most out of it. In order to succeed you must put in some effort and work hard. When you fall you cannot stay down forever. You must get back up.

When I was on the snow at age 15 and age 19 dying I couldn't just lay there and not fight. I had to figure out a way to survive and get back up. It was not easy to fight to survive or even succeed but I did it. After my second accident I did not quit school. I went back and toughed it out and even graduated within 4 years. Although I did not race during the rest of my college years due to the injury I still skied and hung out with friends on the mountain. In order for me to fully recover from my injuries I had to take time off racing but today I am back and ready to go. I will probably never stop skiing because it is my passion. It does not matter if I make the Olympics or if I do not make it because no matter what I am still able to ski. I did not lose the sport I love most.

Your turn: Did you know that although I was in two bad accidents that I wouldn't take them back. I would never turn back time or want to change what happened to me. If you could turn back time would you change anything? Why or why not?

Your turn: So many people in this world suffer. When something bad happens to me and I am down I am reminded that my issues are so much smaller than others. Write about a time when you saw someone who was in a bad situation. It could be anyone from a close friend to the homeless. How did it make you feel to see someone hurting?

Your turn: Write down things that you are thankful for. Why are you thankful for the things you put down?

_____

_____

_____

_____

_____

_____

_____

_____

_____

_____

_____

_____

_____

_____

_____

_____

_____

_____

_____

_____

_____

_____

_____

_____

_____

_____

_____

_____

_____

_____

_____

_____

_____

Your turn: If you could accomplish one thing what would it be? Why do you want to accomplish this thing?

Your turn: During my recovery with both accidents I had a lot of people who cared about me and who were there for me. I owe the people who helped me get my life back on track so much. Write about good things that you have done for others.

Your turn: What kind of person are you now? What type of person do you want to be in the future?

Your turn: All of us have talents. My talent is skiing. What are some of your talents? Maybe you are good at art or math. How can you use your talents in the future?

_____
_____
_____
_____
_____
_____
_____
_____
_____
_____
_____
_____
_____
_____
_____
_____
_____
_____
_____
_____
_____
_____
_____
_____
_____
_____
_____
_____
_____
_____
_____
_____
_____

God Comes First

I was raised a Christian and knowing God and being close him is important to me and my family. Without God I would be lost in my life and I need to have God to guide me and help me when I am having a problem in my life. I also thank God daily for everything that he has done for me and my family. God has given so much to me and I could never thank him enough for everything that he has done to make my life amazing.

No one forced me to believe in God. I chose to believe on my own. Like many, I had moments when I would question my faith or put other things before God. Sometimes I still have doubts or decide not to listen to God but I try my best to always put him first and put everything else, including skiing second. Without God I have nothing and it is important for me to have someone other than family and friends to rely on when it comes to tough decisions.

Some people start thinking about God when something bad is going on, like they are on a bumpy plane or just got in a bad car crash, but this is not a good thing. We must think about God before we are put in a terrible situation because by doing so we can be confident and happy, knowing that we have someone to lean on with every aspect of our lives. Faith in Christ should mean everything to you, not just be important when you are in a life threatening situation.

When I was in my ski accidents I actually did not pray for God to save me. I didn't necessarily want to die but I was fine with whatever God had planned for me. Instead of praying that I would live I prayed that my family would be able to live a normal life with the loss of me. I prayed that my brother would get back up on skis and that my family would not quit doing what they love just because I am no longer with them. Death was not scary to me because I knew that no matter what God was going to take care of me.

I remember the words that I thought to God as I was on the snow dying. "God, please take care of my family when I am gone. Please allow them to move on and live a happy, normal life. I know that they will see me soon Lord. Please take care of them." I thought about my mother who had lost her first husband to a drunk driver. I prayed that she would be able to overcome the loss of me. I didn't want my dad to lose his ski buddy and I didn't want my brother to stop skiing. I wanted my family to be normal and not worry about me, or whether or not I was okay. I was in God's hands after both accidents and I was more than okay. I was great. It wasn't me who needed the prayers. It was my family.

God is the only one that I can truly trust with anything and everything. He will never, ever share a secret or get mad at me for having a rough day. He understands, is forgiving and loving. God has more love for you than your parents, which is amazing to me because I don't know about your parents but mine love me more than I will ever know. When I have a tough decision or something that is really bothering me, and I cannot run to anyone I run towards God.

I am proud of my faith. I am not one to go around and say, "You must believe or else . . ." I just try to treat people like they want to be treated and share my faith through actions. My father always tells me that actions speak louder than words. Anyone can say, "I am a Christian and I believe in God," but when it comes right down to it do they act like Christians? Some do and some don't. I was raised in a home where we do things for others and show kindness through actions. We try to do as Jesus would do but as you know since we are not perfect mistakes do happen.

I also believe that we need to respect each other's beliefs. If you are Jewish or do not even believe in God then that is fine and should be respected. We should not treat each other any different based on our religious beliefs. If you are the type who is more silent about what you believe in then that's great. Whatever you chose to believe in just make sure it is because you want to believe in it and no one is forcing you to believe.

To me God is everything. He is the most important aspect of my life and nothing can or will change that. After my trip to Heaven I really started to believe even more and my belief in God became even stronger. To be honest I did not want to see to believe. I wanted to believe without seeing but it did not happen that way. I do not know why God decided to bring me to Heaven and I probably never will know that answer but one thing I do know is that ever since that day I know where I want to be when I die.

I feel that it is important to give back. My family has always given back to those in need and they have rubbed off on me. Today I am giving to a 3 year old girl in Africa who is in need of fresh food and clean water. Her house is made of mud and sticks and some of the money that I give to her and her family goes towards home repairs as well as schooling and medical needs. Hopefully by just donating a little every month she can have a chance at life.

God writes about giving back to those in need. He says that we should not be selfish but instead selfless. When you die you cannot take your possessions to Heaven, nor do you need to. Instead you should give what you can on Earth so those who are left behind can benefit. If you see a homeless person on the street in the middle of winter don't be afraid to give your coat to them. You probably have a lot of coats, where this person has none. Who knows, by giving up something like a coat you might even save a life. The person that you gave the coat to might not freeze to death but instead live to see another day.

Giving should be a part of your daily life. Instead of seeing what you can do for yourself reach out and see what you can do for others. If you are in a parking lot and see a parking place that is close to the store and you notice an elderly person driving behind you let the elderly person have the spot instead of taking it for yourself. You are young and have strong legs so you should be able to move faster and easier. It is the little things in life that count. If you can make one person's day easier every day then you will find yourself to be a much happier person in the future.

Every day I see people walking around depressed. When I ask them what is wrong they say, "I wish that I had this, or I wish that I could do this thing. I don't know why God didn't allow me to be an athlete." I hear a lot of women complaining about their body types and why they cannot be beautiful. Sometimes even I get caught up in the fact that I am not a stick thin model. What I came to realize is that it is not what we have or don't have that makes us happy. It is what we do with our lives that has a positive impact on others that makes us happy.

We can be the most beautiful person on the outside. We could have the long blonde hair, be 5'10" and 100 pounds. We could be that perfect model or the guy that all of the girls are after but on the inside be unhappy and depressed. If we are not serving God or even doing good for other people then we will never have the chance to be happy. We will stay depressed and down all of the time and never have the opportunity to really make a change.

After my second ski accident I could have stayed down and been like, "Why did this happen again? Why me?" I chose however, to see what God's plan was for me. I wanted to know why I was sent to Heaven and why I came back to Earth. Why did I live? What does God want from me? What am I supposed to do with the gift that God gave me? After the accident the gift that God gave me was being able to see Heaven and actually go into his kingdom. God gave me hope for my future as well as giving me a purpose in life. Although I do not know exactly what God wants me to do in my life I do know that God wants me to be there for others in need and really have an impact in society.

After my accidents I do not remember a time when I actually felt sorry for myself. I never really had the "Why me?" thoughts except when it was with "God what do you want me to do with this?" I never really thought of my situations as a bad thing because I knew that something good would come out of the bad. God promises that good things will come and that he will take the bad and make it good. I just had to wait and see what his plan for me was and for now it is writing my books.

God does amazing things in our lives. He really does give us everything. I know that we always want more because that is how we are as human beings, a little selfish and greedy. God will not always give us exactly what we want but he will give us what we need. If you want long beautiful hair but you do not have it and God is not giving it to you then don't worry about it. Instead try to focus on what God is putting directly in front of you. Try to find the message he is trying to give you and make the most out of what he tells you to do.

The paramedic in the back of the ambulance told me that I can do whatever I want with my life. The police officer told me to hold on and that I will be alright. Basically what I was told during one of the worst times in my life was to never give up. I was told to stay strong and stay positive. These people did not come out and directly say these things to me because they couldn't. When you are dying the last thing you want to hear is stay positive and things will be alright. After I survived I realized what they were really telling me, which is to never give up and to keep moving forward.

God never left me and he put people in my life who were going to help me get back up on my feet and get strong again. He gave me the determination to work hard and the will to get back up on skis. God does not give you blue eyes or long nails or a perfect body just because you want it. Instead he gives you internal gifts such as courage or strength. Every single person has their own, special, unique gifts from God and we must take them and be thankful that he gave them to us.

Your turn: If you could change one thing about the way you look what would it be and why? Why is it so important for you to change this thing about yourself?

_____

_____

_____

_____

_____

_____

_____

_____

_____

_____

_____

_____

_____

_____

_____

_____

_____

_____

_____

_____

_____

_____

_____

_____

_____

_____

_____

_____

_____

_____

_____

_____

_____

_____

Your turn: If you did change this one thing about yourself do you think it would make you happy forever? Why or why not?

Your turn: Self-image is huge in society. When I had my double black eye, skull fracture, neck brace and body cast I looked like a space alien. People were constantly staring at me wondering what had happened. I felt like all eyes were on me and it was uncomfortable. What I learned is that you should be happy with who you are and not worry so much about what other people think.

Are you happy with yourself? Do you think that you could be content with everything about who you are? Why or why not?

Your turn: I really had to put a lot of trust in the people who were saving my life, especially after the second accident. When I was unconscious on the snow with a possible broken neck and a skull fracture there was a lot of pressure on those who were trying to save me. I also had to trust that they would do the right thing for me and not move my neck. It was scary not knowing if I would ever walk again.

Is there someone in your life who you trust with anything? Who can you talk to and trust and know that whatever you say will be protected and guarded? Why is this person so special?

Your turn: Has anyone ever told you a secret and asked you not to say anything? Do not write what the secret was. Did you keep your friend's secret? Why or why not? If you told someone something would you want them telling others?

_____

_____

_____

_____

_____

_____

_____

_____

_____

_____

_____

_____

_____

_____

_____

_____

_____

_____

_____

_____

_____

_____

_____

_____

_____

_____

_____

_____

_____

_____

Your Life

After my second accident a student that I did not know came up to me and said, "Are you the girl that had that bad ski accident?" I looked at her and said, "Yes, I am." She then went on to talk about how she heard some talk around the campus about what had happened to me and that a lot of people know about it. She said that people are amazed that I survived and they are even more surprised that I came back to school to finish up the year. "Thank you for coming back and showing everyone that no matter what circumstances you are in that you can accomplish your goals and live your life," she finally said before walking off.

I later learned that people had been saying that not only is it a miracle that I did not lose my life but it is amazing that I am still trying my hardest to make the most out of my situation. One of my friends said to me one day at lunch, "Aubrie, what made you come back? I mean if I was in your shoes I would have dropped out of the semester and gone home." I told my friend that I did not want to go home and dwell on the fact that I almost lost my ability to walk and that I have seizures and have a hard time focusing due to headaches. I want to be here, studying, where I will have a distraction from everything that happened. There was no way I was going home to feel sorry for myself. This is my life and I am going to make the most out of it, no matter what is thrown my way.

As time went on I would get more and more questions from people. "Aubrie, are you ever going to ski again? Are you afraid to get back up? Are you going to race again? What are you going to do now that you almost died? What was it like to go to Heaven? Can you tell me what happened? Why are you still here and not with your family?" Thousands of questions came at me daily and I would just answer them the best I could. Some questions I could not answer because even I didn't know the answers. Questions such as "Why do you think this happened to you?" and "What do you think God's plan is for you?" were impossible to answer so I would just say, "I do not know."

People were surprised that I did not quit school, even my family was shocked that I decided to go back. My parents did not make me go back to college after the accident. My mother actually wanted me to stay home and drop out for the semester and my dad was nervous sending me back but I said, "I have to go back. I can't let this knock me down." I really liked college and I was not going to miss out on half of my freshman year. There was no way I was going to just quit and give up. I had no choice but to do the best I could in my classes.

When something happens to you do not allow that incident to dictate your life forever. This is your life and you are the one in charge of it. If you want to go to school then go. Don't let anything stop you from achieving your dreams. Everyone gets knocked down and if we all just gave up and did not get back into our lives then we would not have CEO's or Presidents. We would not have stories to tell about overcoming hardships or making it in life. If we all failed and stayed failures then we would have no such thing as success. In order to achieve something great you must learn how to succeed. Overcome your obstacle and figure out a way to make your life the way you have always dreamed it to be.

We all have a story to tell. This story that you are reading is mine but you have one too. Your story is just as great as anyone else's if not better. Get out in the world and experience everything. Take in what you see and hear and learn from your environment. Make your life beautiful and paint it with many colors. One day when you have a family of your own you can tell them of all of your great adventures and be proud of yourself.

Remember that this is your life and whatever decision you make you must live with it forever. Your actions and the things that you choose to do will stick with you forever. I chose not to be knocked down forever but some people just have a difficult time picking themselves back up. There is no rush to get back up but eventually if you want to live a productive life and have meaning in your life then you need to find a way to be happy.

You have so much to look forward to in your life. I know that sometimes it can be difficult to believe that your life will turn out to be great but trust yourself and you will see that you can really live a great life. Hard work in life will bring results so you need to figure out a way to overcome any obstacle and find your purpose in life. When you are doing what you love you will feel proud and good about yourself.

Your turn: I had to have people save my life when I was in my accidents. If no one was there to keep me awake or get me to the hospital I would have been dead. I would not have been here writing this book if it were not for the people who held my head and kept my neck and back still. I wouldn't be here if it were not for the paramedics giving me oxygen and rushing me down the mountain at 15 years old. I had to have physically save me.

Today I do not rely on people to save me or get me out of tough situations because I can save myself. I am the type of person who does not want to wait around for someone to come and fix whatever I have going on. If I can get through my problems with God's help and through my own strength then I learn a lot more about my life and my own abilities.

Write about a situation where you had to figure something out on your own. What did it feel like to be alone? What did you learn from your experience?

_____

_____

_____

_____

_____

_____

_____

_____

_____

_____

_____

_____

_____

_____

_____

_____

_____

_____

_____

Your turn: Why is it important to learn how to do things on your own and not always have someone come to your rescue?

Your turn: Talk about a time when you had someone step in and rescue you. How did it feel to have someone bail you out of a situation? Did you learn anything from it?

Being Young

At 15 I learned that no one lives forever. When the ski patrol stopped the sled and ran up to me halfway down the mountain they were concerned that I was going to stop breathing and die right then and there. I was spitting up blood and they did not know where it was coming from, making it difficult to tell if I was going into shock or if this was just something minor.

This time in my life was also scary for me because I did not really get a chance to say goodbye to my brother, who took off right after I was put in the sled. There was nothing Austin could do and I couldn't even see him because of all of the people around me. I was scared that I wasn't going to see him again. What if I didn't even make it to the hospital to see my dad? I learned real quick the importance of family and sticking together and being kind to each other that day.

After my second accident when I was 19 I almost did not get to see my mom or dad before I went to Heaven. My parents were actually looking for me because I never came down the mountain. I never finished the race so they knew that something was wrong. I remember for a split second I heard my dad's voice. I do not remember what he said but I remember seeing his yellow jacket. My mom was next to him, with her red jacket but everything was such a blur.

I was passing out a lot and the ski patrol did not think that I was even going to live long enough to get to the hospital. My parents of course did not know the severity of my injuries until they were told by someone at the top of the race course, then again at the hospital. I almost died and if I would have died my parents would have been left with "She was too young." We never even got the chance to say goodbye."

Being young is great. Your whole world is open and you can literally do whatever you want. You can have big dreams and ambitions and you are healthy with few if any medical issues. Your world is for you to explore and you should be able to basically be carefree and not have too many responsibilities. What many youth fail to realize is that they are not invincible. When you are young you think that nothing can hurt you and you cannot die because God doesn't take young people. Well, I was only 15 the first time God almost took me and I was 19 the second.

While you are young you should focus on God first, if you are a Christian, and even if you are not a Christian and you want to get to know God then you should focus on him and have him come first. Next you should be good to your family and let them know that you love them. Tell them what you want out of your life and ask them to support you. They might think that your dreams are too big but who cares. This is your life and you are young so you should think huge.

The last thing is to live. Live like every day is your last because you never know, it very well could be. I do not want to sound like the grim reaper but young people do die. There was a 13 year old girl that I raced against who died when she got hit by a snowmobile in Vail. No one was expecting that to happen and it was devastating. Another girl that I went to high school died while racing a friend down the mountain at Keystone. She struck a tree and crushed her chest. She was only 14.

Things do happen so just know that your actions affect your life. If you want to live a good life and have people respect you and if you want to be happy then choose wisely. Never give into peer pressure just because you think you will look better or be cool. Just be you because you are good enough. Live the life you have always dreamed of living and enjoy every single minute of it. Learn from your mistakes and just make the most out of a bad situation.

After my first accident at 15 years old I was asked by my classmates, "Will you ever race again? What will happen if you cannot get back up and race? How will this affect your life? Are you happy even though you can no longer ski?" My reply to all of these questions was I will make the most out of what I have and enjoy the life that I have left. God has given me a second chance to live and I want to see what I can do to make it great. I want to now live every day like it is my last.

Your turn: "When our will is weak, when our thinking is confused, and when our conscience is burdened with a load of guilt, we must remember that God cares for us continually; his compassion never fails," (Hosea 14:3-8). When I was recovering from my injuries in both accidents I became confused as to what I was supposed to do with my life. "God, what do you want me to do with this?" I often wondered what my purpose in life was now that I was out of skiing and racing.

When I was weak after having seizures, and being exhausted after my head injury during my second fall, God was the one who gave me strength. He never let me lose sight of my dreams of getting back up on skis and getting back on the race course. His compassion was amazing and he turned all of the bad into good. Because of God I was able to pick myself back up and get back to what I love most.

What are some things that you are burdened with? What confuses you most about your life? When you have negative feelings and feel that you are going to fail what do you do to overcome your feelings of shame and guilt?

_____

_____

_____

_____

_____

_____

_____

_____

_____

_____

_____

_____

_____

_____

Your turn: What do you want to do with your life before you graduate high school? What are some things that you want to accomplish before you go to college?

When I was 17 I wrote my first book, "A New Beginning: Fighting to get back up on Skis." It was a huge accomplishment and when I went to college I already had my book into a publisher. You can do big things with your life, even when you are young. You can do anything that you put your mind to.

Facing Your Fears

After my ski accidents I was forced to face my fears. I had a lot of fears. During my second accident I feared that I would never walk again. I also feared that I would never be able to finish college due to my head injury. My arm was broken pretty bad and I was afraid that it would not heal right or that I might not have full use of it. After my second fall my right knee was also broken. It was the same knee that I injured at 15, during my first accident. Would I be okay? Would I live to see another day?

After I recovered after both of my accidents I had fears of never being able to ski again. That fear was bigger after my second accident because I had a severe head injury. Would I have seizures forever? Would I be able to even drive again? There was even a point where I was not allowed to drive due to the severity of my injuries.

When it came to sports after both of my accidents I was afraid that I would not be able to perform like I use to. I was a good, strong athlete but because of my lung injury at 15 years old and my head and neck injury at 19 years old I feared that I would not be able to go for a run without being in pain. "Will I ever be normal again?" I would ask myself as I struggled to get back up to normal activities. The biggest fear of all was the fact that I might never ski again. During my recovery I really didn't care if I could no longer race but I did care about not skiing ever again.

I can tell you that it was not easy getting back up on skis. I did have moments where I would have to stop in the middle of a run and calm my thoughts. Flashbacks of my accidents came frequently and it was difficult getting back in the gates after my second fall. I can tell you that I will never race at Winter Park again because it would bring back too much. I cannot go back on the course at Winter Park due to what happened there. Actually, I have not skied at Winter Park since that day.

What I learned from all of my fears is that in order for me to overcome them I must face them. Some fears however, I cannot face. Racing at Winter Park is something that I just cannot do again, and that is okay. I had to overcome a lot just to get back on my skis and even get back in the gates. At 15 years old I was not racing in the gates. I was free skiing when I fell. Sometimes when I go past the place where I wiped out I still have memories of that day and I just have to shake it off and move on.

When you have a fear you must try to push it out of your mind and get past it. Sometimes fear is good and fear can save your life. There are times though when you must realize that your fears are small and just face them. If you never try or you allow yourself to fear then you will not experience life. In order to live you must try new things and get back up where you left off.

A couple years ago I received an email from a young female wanting me to help her overcome her fear of skiing. She read my story over the internet and decided to email me. This girl was coming out to Colorado from Texas for a family vacation and she really wanted to try skiing but was afraid that she would get hurt. After she read what happened to me her fear of skiing grew. In her email she asked me why I got back up after both accidents and why I did not quit. She wanted to know how I overcame my fears of the mountain and the sport.

I emailed her back and told her that I learned how to ski when I was 2 years old and though all of my years skiing I have fallen a lot. Most of the time I do not get more than a bump and I am able to pick myself back up with no problems. Falls are part of the sport and it is unlikely that a new beginner will get injured. I told her that she should try skiing because if she doesn't she will go home wondering what it was like. She would even be a little disappointed in herself for not giving it a try.

I do not know what happened to this girl or if she did try skiing. I hope she gave it a go and faced her fears. In life you must take a chance and try something new. If it does not work out then that does not mean that you failed. Every new experience that you have just makes you a better, stronger, happier person, even if the experience is negative.

Journal Entry

08/04/10

"Our troubles should cause us to cling tightly to God, not attempt to bargain our way out of pain. We can thank and praise God for what he has already done for us, and for his love and mercy," (Bible).

This is one of my favorite quotes from Jonah. Sometimes I find myself trying to bargain myself out of pain and I forget that God is the one who is trying to put the pieces back together. Getting back up on the race course is extremely difficult and I often wonder if will ever be as good as I use to be. Will I ever be able to be as strong as I was before the accidents?

Everyone says that because of my head injury racing is dangerous for me. I should just free ski and that is even dangerous. I realize that one more head injury and I will be dead but that is the risk that I must take. It is probably not too smart of me to get back up but I am not afraid. I am not afraid to fall again or get hurt again. Skiing is a dangerous sport, like most sports are. Injuries are just part of playing and having fun.

In order to succeed one must take a risk. When I was ski instructing I would see many people stiffen up and freeze when they saw the hill they were going to learn on. They were so afraid to learn how to ski, even with someone there helping them. The thing is they were all facing their fears. Some of the people I had taught had never seen snow before and they were not use to the cold or the elevation. When I got them on the hill and their skis started to move they were scared.

I am so glad that I had the opportunity to teach skiing because I learned more than my clients. Most of my clients were from out of town and nervous. They had careers at home and could not afford to injure themselves. Each and every one of them had to put a lot of trust in me, that I would keep them safe. I remember one female was so afraid that she started to cry and I had to tell her that everything would be alright and that she was going to have fun.

I also learned how to have patients when I was an instructor. I love to ski fast and go down the steep bumps and fly off jumps. I sometimes even ski out of bounds and love the powder. The terrain that I ski is very difficult and you must know exactly what you are doing or you are going to get seriously injured or even killed. Because of my talent and where I spend most of my hours on the slopes I sometimes get annoyed when I have to stay on the easy runs all day in a wedge. It is frustrating when there is fresh powder and you are stuck teaching a beginner on the groomed runs.

I had to learn how to have patients and compassion as well as stay professional. If I complained about how I couldn't ski the runs I like to ski then the customer who is trying to enjoy his/her vacation is not going to be happy. I was forced to put myself in their shoes and treat them like I would want to be treated or have my family treated if they were learning a new sport.

God really does amazing things in people's lives. Every day I would wake up in the freezing cold, go up and teach beginners all day. I would give up my fun and free time to teach those who wanted to learn a new sport. There were many days when I would look up at the top of the mountain and just wish that I was up there on the steep stuff. I even prayed to God and asked him to give me expert skiers, but he never did. I was always stuck with the beginners.

As time went by I realized that God was teaching me a lesson. The lesson I learned was love. God taught me a new love for skiing and he taught me how to appreciate what I have. I grew up with a family of skiers and I had the opportunity to ski almost daily during the ski season. When I was teaching beginners to ski they always said, "I wish that I started at a young age," and "You are so lucky that you have all of this." Hearing these comments amazed me and

I felt so blessed to have not only the beautiful mountains but also the sport of skiing.

As time went by I realized that I loved teaching skiing. I no longer really longed to be on the steep runs because sharing the sport I love most all the sudden became important. I learned that giving back is a great feeling and teaching a little kid how to have fun and giving a kid hope is the best gift of all. Watching people smile as they understand how to turn and move on the snow was so amazing and a blessing from God.

I truly am blessed to have all of these opportunities in my life. My dad and grandfather really did give me a lot to look forward to. I am so happy and thankful that I have a supportive and wonderful family who loves sports and who is into fitness and exercise. If it was not for my family giving me every single opportunity and supporting me with everything that I do I would be lost in this world. I wouldn't be the person I am today if it was not for my family.

It is August and another ski season is around the corner. As I write this I can feel the skis beneath my feet. I can feel the grip of the snow as my ski is put on edge. I can imagine the turns and the speed. The air is cold and numbs my face. I cannot wait for another season and hope that is just as good as the last.

I am also going to keep teaching my friends and little cousins to ski because I want to share this sport with others. It is so much fun when you are up there with your friends, giving them a dream come true. One of my friends wanted to learn how to ski so bad and I took her up. She did awesome and I would like to go with her again next season. She loved it and wants to go again.

I also taught a friend of mine to snowboard. We went several times and plan on going again. He did great his first and second day and was even on more difficult runs by the end of his third day. A family friend of ours has a son and I took him snowboarding and by the end of his first day he was doing bumps and jumps. I also got him up on my snow skates and he just jumped on and went. I'd like to see him board more too. He is so talented and athletic.

Sports are a big part of my life, not just skiing but every sport. You name it, I play it. I believe that people should do what they love, whether that be sports or music. Having hobbies and being interested in stuff is what makes us unique. Every person has a talent, and they should explore it and use it to not only benefit them but others as well.

Your turn: Have you ever seen the MTV show MADE? I have watched several episodes and my favorite was of a girl who was into music who learned to surf. She even did well in her competition. Have you ever thought about trying something new? If you could do one thing that you normally would not do what would it be, and why?

_____

_____

_____

_____

_____

_____

_____

_____

_____

_____

_____

_____

_____

_____

_____

_____

_____

_____

_____

_____

_____

_____

_____

_____

_____

_____

_____

_____

_____

_____

_____

_____

_____

The best I can be

I wish that I could say that I just hop on a pair of skis and that is all that it takes to compete and ski well every day. I wish that it was just that easy but the truth is that it takes a lot of work and preparing. During the off season I have to come up with a work-out routine so I can stay in shape for the up-coming season, which can be a challenge.

My routine during the off season is to run, run, run, lift weights and work with a coach. I also have a ski machine that trains my leg muscles that I use during skiing. My personal trainer and coach help out big time when it comes to a routine. Without the help from a professional I would not be able to be a strong competitor.

There are days when I do not want to get out of bed at 6:00 in the morning to go for a run but I realize that in order for me to stay healthy and in shape I need to focus on my routine and stay focused. Every day I wake up between 6:00 and 6:30 and I am in the gym by 7:00ish to go to what I call my personal boot camp.

When I get up in the morning I am not only helping myself stay in shape and prepared. I am also helping my family. My parents say that because of me getting up first thing in the morning to work out that I am inspiring them to do the same. My mother is not a morning person. She never has been but when she sees me pushing myself in the gym and really staying focused on being the best that I can be she gets up and works out as well. My mother and father both push themselves because they want to keep me focused and get healthy themselves.

Life is not easy and staying in shape for skiing is not either. The thing is that if everything was easy and given to us we would not benefit from it. There would be no such thing as learning or working to succeed. Our lives would be dull and boring. I am glad that I have to work to earn what I have because if I didn't I wouldn't have appreciation for anything.

In your life just be the best you can be. I know that there is a lot of peer pressure and pressure for you to be perfect and look a certain way. In order to fit in you must dress in a cool way, possibly smoke and drink but if you chose to do activities that are not good for you make sure you are doing them because you want to, not because you feel pressured to do so.

I remember being teased a little and mocked for not getting into drugs or drinking but I chose not to put harmful substances in my body. Harmful substances also include certain foods, such as fried, or fast food. I always ate organic or very healthy foods because I couldn't afford to get sick or throw away all of my hard work. When my friends were eating cheese burgers I was eating fruit and veggies. Sometimes I would get made fun of for not eating like everyone else but in the end I was glad that I chose not to give in to what my peers wanted me to do.

I can only be me. There is no way that I could be someone else because I am Aubrie, not so and so across the street. During winter break a lot of people come to Colorado, especially Breckenridge because it is a family resort. Often I see visitors trying to be speed skiers when they do not know what they are doing. They lose sight of the fact that they are not at an Olympic level or even at an advanced or expert level. When they lose sight of their ability it becomes dangerous and people actually get killed.

The same goes for you. If you are trying to be someone you are not you are going to lose sight of who you are and you are not going to find your talents and abilities. You are not going to be able to grow as a person and this can be dangerous. Some people get caught up in the fact that they do not like themselves and want to be like their favorite athlete or singer that they literally lose themselves in the process of trying to be someone else.

I have seen people get caught up in drugs and alcohol because they just cannot find themselves. They have tried to be someone else for so long that they literally end up dying inside. Do not let this be you. Stay who you are because God made you special. You are beautiful in God's eyes and he has a special plan for your life. If you are the best that you can be then that is good enough. No one can tell you who to be, nor should they. You are unique and have a very special purpose in life.

After my second accident I actually went into a deep depression because I was lost and did not know where to turn to or what to do. My face was swollen and my skull was fractured. I was having seizures and I was anything but normal. I remember stuttering and to this day I have a difficult time getting my thoughts out when I speak about my journey back on skis. All of this took a toll on my life and I had to come to realize that I was special and that God was going to use my story to benefit others. I had to believe and hold on to the hope that one day something good would come out of this.

Instead of losing myself in drugs and alcohol, which I could have done, especially after the second accident when I was in college, I decided to just find myself and figure out who I really was. I needed to find a purpose for my life after the accidents and find myself all over again. What I found was that I had more strength that I ever would have realized before my accidents. I learned that I am able to push through any circumstance and learn how to be happy all over again. The biggest lesson that I learned is that life is worth living and that I love myself for who I am. I am content with being me.

Life is a journey and to get through it you need to be content with yourself. Take all of the positive things that you have about yourself and use it. Love yourself and try hard not to think about what you do not have. Everyone is built different. We all have different hair colors and styles. Our bodies are different and the way we act, think, and even breathe is different. Think of it this way. If we were all the same then life would not be interesting. Our world would be boring if we were all perfect and never had flaws. For this reason it is important to take what God has given you and make the most out of it.

Effects on others

I think a lot about how the accidents have affected those around me. When bad things happen you are not the only one who is affected. After the paramedics got to me during both of my accidents they were all affected. Those who witnessed the crash were terrified and thought that I had died. My family did not know if I was going to survive or if they were going to have to bury their daughter.

When I was in my second accident at 19 years old the ski patrol literally jumped from the chair to get to me faster. I was in such bad shape that they could not wait until they got to the top of the chair to get to me and therefore, had to jump. Luckily for them, it was not a big drop to reach me. They were unsure if I was even going to make it to the hospital alive, let alone off the mountain. I was in extremely rough shape and had blood coming out of my ears.

I was not supposed to survive that second accident. Actually, I should have been dead during both of my accidents but my second one was the one that really, actually pretty much killed me. The paramedics during the first accident had their hands full with me to keep me alive as well. They had to keep me awake and talking. They also had to make sure my airway stayed clear with the blood coming up, out of my mouth.

Not only were the rescue workers affected but my friends, teammates, family and even the school that I was attending was affected by what happened to me. My family keeps a lot in. They do not really talk about what happened to me because they do not want to get upset. When people think about what I went through it takes a toll on them and it is hard to go back and relive the nightmare. My family and friends almost lost me and because of it is difficult for them to think about what would have happened if I would have passed away.

When something bad happens to you it is not only happening to you. Those around you are concerned and they are pleading to God that you recover and get out of your situation. Your loved ones and friends care about you and want the best for you. It is important to think about them when you are in a situation because they are going through all kinds of emotions and this takes a lot out of them. Just realize that your friends and family will react to your situation and their emotions are normal. You should try to comfort them as much as you can and let them know that you will somehow pull through and be there for them.

Your turn: Write about a time when your family was concerned for you. What was the emotional toll on you and your loved ones?

_____
_____
_____
_____
_____
_____
_____
_____
_____
_____
_____
_____
_____
_____
_____
_____
_____
_____
_____
_____
_____
_____
_____
_____
_____
_____
_____
_____
_____
_____
_____
_____
_____
_____

Your turn: How do you deal with stress?

Your turn: What are some things that stress you out? Why are they so stressful?

_____

_____

_____

_____

_____

_____

_____

_____

_____

_____

_____

_____

_____

_____

_____

_____

_____

_____

_____

_____

_____

_____

_____

_____

_____

_____

_____

_____

_____

_____

_____

_____

_____

_____

_____

_____

_____

Your turn: Write about a time when you accomplished something great.

Your turn: Write about a time when someone was proud of you. What did you do to make them proud?

Your turn: write about what it is like to be you. Who are you? What makes you, you?

Aubrie freeskiing in Mt. Hood Oregon

Aubrie and her dad Peter at a
Giant Slalam race in Beaver Creek

Aubrie is the first competitor on
the race course in Breckenridge, CO

Aubrie in training, Breckenridge CO

Aubrie training with Quantum
Sports Club, Breckenridge CO

Aubrie and her brother Austin
skiing at age 3, Breckenridge CO

Aubrie and Austin having fun on a
beautiful winter day in Breckenridge

Aubrie and her family. This is the last time that
Aubrie's grandfather, Steve, skied. He is
about 80 years old in this photo.

Aubrie at age 5 after she won her first race
through the program Breckenridge Bombers

When there is no snow: Aubrie gets ready
to go out with friends for a skiing benefit

Hope

Everyone hopes that they will succeed and do something great in their lives. We all want to be the person that others look up to. We hold on to hope and the good that the future will bring in our lives. After my accidents I really wanted to get back up on skis. I was devastated that I might lose the sport that I love and also possibly lose my other goals such as getting a college degree.

I remember feeling down and my whole world was turned upside down. I had no clue where to go from here or what my future was going to have in store for me. What am I supposed to do now that everything is gone? I would ask myself. There would be times where I would cry, wanting someone to comfort me and tell me that everything was going to work out. I just wanted to be reassured that I was going to make it.

After my second accident I learned that I need to pick myself up and go for my goals. I needed to keep fighting if I was going to get a good education and make it in this world. No one could do it for me, nor did I want them to. I realized that this is my life and I am going to make the most out of it and do the best I can. I had already survived my accidents and now I can survive whatever else is thrown my way.

Some people would feel sorry for me. They would feel bad that I was injured so bad and that I almost died. I did have a lot of help but eventually I realized that feeling sorry for myself was not a good thing. I had to do something to become happy and gain fulfillment in my life. I decided to take my life day by day and cherish what

I had, and not dwell so much on what I lost. Soon I learned that by focusing on the positive I am able to live a better life that is not filled with fear and grief.

Life does have surprises. I never thought that I would be an author or even be a speaker about God and how to better your life. I never imagined that the accidents I was in would give other people who are in rough situations hope. When bad things happen we do not understand why or even know what the outcome will be, but we must hold on to hope for a bright future if we are going to get through these bumps in the road.

Did you know that people who have hope tend to be happier? They also tend to have a belief in a higher power, and they are more enthusiastic about life as well as more energetic. People who believe that their lives are going to be great are more likely to succeed and bounce back up after a failure or incident. People who have hope are determined and persistent. They rarely cave in and give up.

Hope brings power in people's lives. Without hope we are hopeless as well as helpless. I know someone who is like me. This person never had ski accidents that almost killed her. She never went through an event that basically took her life. Instead, she went through some rough family situations and believes that everything has to be handed to her. She is unable to move past the negative aspects in her life and move on to bigger and better things. This woman basically lost all hope and gave up.

Like me, this woman has failed over, and over. She has failed so many times that she now believes that nothing good will come her way. She is hopeless and does not want to even try to put the pieces back together. Let me tell you that I understand how she feels. There were and still are days when I feel that I do not want to get up and push forward but I have no choice.

Being happy means having a fulfilling life and obtaining a fulfilling life means having hope for a better future. One must move on and pick themselves up to succeed. I don't care if I have to pick myself up thousands of times. I am going to do whatever it takes to succeed. This is what hope is, being able to look into the future and try your best to reach your goals.

If you are lost in life it is normal. Every single person gets lost and does not know what their purpose is at one point in their lives. After my ski accidents I realized that I might never be an Olympic skier and I might never ski again. I was terrified but I realized that God has a plan for my life and I need to trust him and his timing. Rushing into something and getting into things too fast, before I know what I am supposed to do will set me back even further.

When I was going through my recovery after both accidents of course I was down and devastated but I realized that happiness is a choice. I could have decided to stay down and be depressed forever or I could put a smile on my face, even if things were bad and at least pretend to be happy. You can create your own destiny and you are in charge of how your story is told. I suggest making your story have many colors and paint your picture beautiful.

Your turn: What gives you hope? What does hope mean to you?

Your turn: Did you know that you are very powerful? You have the power to control your own destiny. If you are living in a bad part of town where you have to worry about being shot you can still make the most out of your situation. You can still get past all of the negative things in your life.

If you are going through a tough time or you live in a rough area what are some things you can do to make it out alive and well? How can you make your future bright?

_____

_____

_____

_____

_____

_____

_____

_____

_____

_____

_____

_____

_____

_____

_____

_____

_____

_____

_____

_____

_____

_____

_____

_____

_____

Your turn: God has a plan for you. He wants you to do great things in your life. Every single person on this earth matters and has an opportunity to really make a difference in the lives of those around them. God gave you many talents that no one else has and he wants you to use them for the good of those around you.

What can you do to be happy and make sure that you are using all of the gifts that God gave you? How are you going to succeed in your life?

Your turn: When I was lying on the snow after both accidents I could hear the ski patrol say, "Aubrie, stay with us. Come on, keep your eyes open." They were concerned and did not want to lose me. No one wanted to have to tell my family that I was not coming home because that is such a difficult thing to do.

The people who were saving my life were so compassionate and they really wanted me to live. No one gave up on me, or made me feel uncomfortable. I felt safe with the strangers who were poking me with needles and hooking me up to machines. Their actions made me realize that not all people in this world are bad. There is good on Earth. Because of their actions towards me I decided to put up a fight and live to see another day.

"Our ultimate hope is when we are experiencing terrible illness, persecution, or pain is the realization that this life is not all there-there is life after death. Knowing that we will live forever with God in a place without sin and suffering can help us live above the pain that we face in this life," (Corinthians 4:18).

When I was dying after the second accident I did see Heaven. I went there and felt what it will be like when I am no longer on this earth. Being in Heaven made me want to be a better person on Earth, so when my time comes for real I will be able to be with God forever.

When I came back to Earth I realized that I needed to change my attitude and be someone that people will want to be around. Sometimes I still find myself getting angry at others or being a pill but I try hard not to. I try to treat people how I would want to be treated. I even started to pray for those who do not like me that they will be able to get over their problems and live good lives. Every day I try to be a better Christian and it is not always easy.

What kinds of things do you do to be a good person? How do you treat those around you? Do you get angry in the car when someone cuts you off? Do you curse and give the finger? Are you the type of

person who talks ill about someone behind their back? How do you
think your actions affect those around you?

12/10/2004

Journal entry

I am so glad that I was able to fight and get back up on skis. Not only am I able to ski again, I am able to race too. I am so lucky to have a family who loves and supports me with everything that I want to do in my life. My family means so much to me and I do not know what I would do without them. I am just thrilled that all of my hard work paid off and now I am able to have a second chance at life.

"It is easy to lose heart and quit. We all have faced problems in our relationships or in our work that have cause us to want to think about laying down the tools and walking away," (Corinthians 4:16). There were times when I have thought about just walking away and giving up but I decided that I need to push through and see what God has in store for me.

I believe that hard work brings success. We can be successful in our work or in the way we treat others. Every day can be a success if you want it to be. I learned that through all of my pain and hardships over the past few months that nothing is easy and one must work hard in order to persevere. Through hard work there are rewards and my reward is being able to ski once again. I will never quit skiing, ever.

Every day I thank God for everything that he has done for me. He is my strength and is the one who guides my life. God has done so many wonderful things and I could never thank him enough. I love God and I know that he loves me. God actually loves all of us and I am so thankful for all of the wonderful opportunities he has given me and my family. I really am blessed.

"Our troubles should not diminish our faith or disillusion us. We should realize that there is purpose in our suffering," (Corinthians 4:17). I do not know why God put me in a position to almost die and lose everything but I do know that he wants me to benefit from what happened. God wants me to learn something and do something special with what happened. There is a plan for all of us and only God knows exactly what is in store. I am excited to see what else God has planned for my life and I want to serve him and try to be the best person I can be.

Giving

God says that "A giving attitude is more important than the amount given. The person who can give only a small gift shouldn't be embarrassed. God is concerned about how a person gives from his or her resources," (Corinthians 9:7). After my second accident I found that giving back is important. Actually, God comes first in my life, then giving next.

I feel so blessed and lucky that I have the opportunity to live my life. I almost died twice and now I have a life to live. It is important for me to give back to my community and world because I feel that I have everything that anyone could ever want or need. I have plenty, more than enough. My family has a lot as well and we do give a lot to charity and the church. My parents have taught me that giving to those in need is important because we need to support each other, even those who are strangers.

The people who saved me gave me the gift of life. They did not have to respond to my call for help. No one had to take the time and go the extra mile to make sure I was comfortable and not hurting too bad. The ski patrol did not have to make people leave the scene so I could have more privacy. Because of the actions of the paramedics and even law enforcement I was able to have another chance at life and my family was also given the gift of not having to bury their child.

Today I am giving to a little girl in Africa. I send her and her family money on a monthly basis. This year, 2011, I decided to give up all of my birthday gifts because I want the money that was going to go towards my birthday to go to those in need. Instead of buying me gifts or sending me money my family decided to give money to a family or a good cause. I have so much and giving to someone who has nothing is the best gift of all.

Giving freely and generously is the only way to be happy. If you are selfish with your money or things then you cannot make someone else feel good and be happy. By making others happy and serving those in need, you will be happy too. When you give, even if it is just a little, you have a purpose to get up in the morning. You are not as likely to become depressed and your selfish needs will go away. In return you will become a better person, a person who others look up to.

I feel that I could never give enough. I have so much and I am so grateful that my life was spared. I could never thank God enough for everything that he has done in my life. Personally, I find purpose when I am assisting a homeless person by feeding them or giving clothing away. I am so fortunate to have the opportunity to support a child in Africa, a country where I have never been. Since the accidents so many opportunities have opened up and my world has become much better. My life is full of great things and I couldn't ask for anything better.

I have heard people say, "Aubrie I want to give to a child too but I do not have the money or time." I hear people talk about how they cannot volunteer because they are too busy. Well if you are too busy to volunteer that is fine. There are other ways in which a person can give back besides giving money or time.

God wants you to be creative when you are giving to someone. Giving can be in the form of assisting someone with directions or just by telling the truth when you mess up. Giving is a way of telling someone you care and if the only way you can give is by being a kind person and not talking bad about others then that is great. It is a start. Just do what you can and always look for new opportunities to give.

When you decide to start giving back to society try not to compare what you are giving to what others are giving. Giving is not a competition and should not be used as a way to make yourself look better in the eyes of others. When you give back make sure you are doing it for the right reasons. Give because you want to, not because you feel the need to impress people. When you give freely and not ask for anything in return that is when you will really learn a lot about yourself and others.

I have learned that people are amazing. There was a little girl that I saw in Hawaii while I was vacationing there. She had extremely bad arthritis and could not really do much. Her pain was so bad that she had to be carried everywhere and had difficulty walking. I felt very bad for her and really wanted to help her but there was nothing that I could do.

Well, this girl wanted to go swimming in the ocean. Due to her pain she was not really able to move her limbs and I watched her struggle to make it to the water. This child's father was close behind her, ready to assist if needed. When her toes hit the water I noticed a huge smile on her face. She looked up at her dad and a look of pure joy was on her face. Her dad assisted her in the water and she was able to swim in the ocean for the first time.

What this little girl had that many people do not have is grace. Although she was in pain she was still able to show those around her that anything is possible. This child taught me to be even more thankful that I only had a few short term injuries and that I did not have to deal with an illness or even life-long pain. I also learned that everyone has goals that they want to accomplish and no matter who we are we can always give something daily, even if it is hope and thanks.

Your turn: Do you know someone who could use your help? Do you know of anyone who would benefit from the gift of giving? If so, who? How can you help them?

_____

_____

_____

_____

_____

_____

_____

_____

_____

_____

_____

_____

_____

_____

_____

_____

_____

_____

_____

_____

_____

_____

_____

_____

_____

_____

_____

_____

_____

_____

_____

_____

_____

Your turn: Did you know that if you gossip about your friends that you will lose their friendships? Do you know anyone who gossips a lot? How does it make you feel when you hear someone say something negative about someone else?

Your turn: Did you know that every action has results? Write about how your actions affect your life.

Your turn: Who is your hero? Why do you look up to this person?

_____

_____

_____

_____

_____

_____

_____

_____

_____

_____

_____

_____

_____

_____

_____

_____

_____

_____

_____

_____

_____

_____

_____

_____

_____

_____

_____

_____

_____

_____

_____

_____

_____

_____

_____

_____

Moving Forward

It was not easy for me to move on after my accidents, especially after my 2nd accident. A couple days after my second accident my parents sent me back to school. Going back was my choice but my parents regret even allowing me to make that choice. They still wish that they would have kept me home. No one, not even me, knew the extent of my injuries and what I would have to learn how to do all over again.

During both accidents I had to learn how to walk again. After both falls my right knee was messed up, and physical therapy was a pain, literally. I had to learn how to balance and even put my right leg in front of my left, which was difficult and painful. I even had to learn how to ski with a huge brace and even adjust my stance enough to keep my knee from hurting on the race course.

After my second accident I was skiing with one arm for a while. I really wanted to get to Nationals so as soon as I could I was back up on the race course, even against the doctor's orders. Skiing with one arm is difficult but when you are trying to race and cannot balance yourself with both of your arms, it is nearly impossible. On top of that I also had a fractured skull, neck and a fractured knee. Try getting up on skis with that and it is tough.

I was determined though to make Nationals and I was going to do whatever it took to do it. I do not know how I made it but somehow I was able to get back up and perform. I remember my coach trying to give me advice on how to race with one arm. "Aubrie," he said, "I know that it is difficult to do this with one arm but you are doing great. Try to use your left arm for balance and really use your legs to hold you up. You can do this. You'll figure it out."

During my training runs I found it extremely difficult to find my balance and actually figure out a way to make the gates and not be so late coming into it. I literally tried everything from turning last minute to trying to turn early and nothing seemed to work. I was not performing and getting the lines that I usually do. I just could not figure out how to move my skis the right way. The power that I had before the accident seemed to be gone and I kept blowing out of the course.

Finally, I got the hang of skiing with one arm. Somehow I figured out how to position my body and get through the gates without messing up. When my coaches and father thought that I was ready to get back up in a competition they allowed me to do so. It took a lot of work for me to even be able to race again and everyone thought that I was out for good after that second crash.

I remember my first day back to competing. It was a beautiful, warm day. My arm was still in a cast, useless, and my leg was still in a huge brace. I remember the stares from the other competitors as I reached the race arena. There were some whispers as well but everyone was nice people were not pointing and laughing. Instead they were supportive and glad to see that I was up and doing well.

"Hey Aubrie, do you remember me?" It was the girl from the DU ski team, the girl that I had talked to right before my accident. "Yes, how are you?" I asked. She gave me a hug and said, "We are glad to have you back. I am glad that you are alright. I hope you do well today." After people started to recognize who I was they came up to me and told me how glad they are to see me out and that they are glad that I survived. People were shocked that I even came back to racing. "If that was me I wouldn't ever go in another course again," I heard someone say.

When it was my turn to race the man at the start said, "Good luck out there. You will do great this time. Congratulations on getting back up." I did do well in that race and even qualified for nationals. My team and I placed 5th in Nationals. After nationals I was forced to take the rest of the season off to recover and rest. It was going to be a long road to recovery but I was going to be alright and make it through.

Moving forward is not always easy. It takes a lot of patients and courage to move on after something bad happens to you. In order to move forward you need to be dedicated and motivated, which at times seems to be impossible. There were many times when I actually quit and gave up, only to get back up again. I remember saying to myself, "I do not want to do this anymore. Life is so hard and I cannot get up. I just can't seem to overcome this." It wasn't until I started to see God's plan for me that I realized that the world is open and I can do whatever I want.

One day my mother read my first book, "A New Beginning: fighting to get back up on Skis," and she said to me, "Aubrie, why not publish this? You can really help a lot of people by getting your story out. I think you should try to get published." That is what I did. I am writing today because my mother inspired me to share with others that reaching your dreams really can happen. My mom is the reason that I achieved yet another goal.

After people heard about my story they started wanting me to speak about how to persevere. I have talked to a few groups of people as well as individuals. Some people on the mountain recognize me as the girl who almost died. I have had some people come up to me who have never skied before and said, "Because of you I am going to try skiing. I am so glad that you got back up." I have had the opportunity to teach people that you really can rise above and enjoy life.

One day I received an email from a woman through my website www.aubriemindock.zoomshare.com. This woman was from Florida and coming out to visit for a couple of weeks. Her first stop was going to be Breckenridge. Next she was going to go to Keystone and Vail. This woman had never seen snow or even been to a ski resort. She had never been to Colorado or anywhere near the mountains during the summer. The letter read:

Thank you for sharing your story. I will be visiting Colorado for the first time next week. One of my biggest fears is snow skiing. I am afraid of having something attached to my feet and moving down the snow at a fast pace. I also have a fear of heights. Getting to the top of the mountain is going to be a scary experience for me.

The reason I am writing you is because you encouraged me to give skiing a try. After I read your story I realized that life is too short. I am sorry for what you went through but I am glad that you had the strength and courage to get back up. You are amazing and an inspiration. Because of you, I am going to face my fears and not run from them. I want to know what it is like to ski so I am going to try.

I hope to see you in the Olympics one day. If you make it and decide that you still want to be an Olympic athlete I will be rooting for you. Good luck in your future. May it be bright and full of love and happiness.

From,

Anonymous (I will not state her name).

People from all over the United States emailed me saying that they are glad that I was able to move forward and do what I love most. If I had the chance to go back to those two days and not have gone out skiing I wouldn't change a thing. I am glad that the accidents happened because now I have the opportunity to touch more people than I would have before the accidents. I am able to reach out and share my experience with thousands of people who need encouragement.

The best gift of all came from my accidents. Today I am doing great and I have everything that a girl could ever want. My family is super supportive and encouraging and the best part is that I am able to give strength, hope and love to those who need it. My life couldn't get much better than it is right now, today. Moving forward opened up all kinds of new opportunities and allowed me to focus less on the past and more on the awesome things that are to come.

I have been asked about dating and guys quite often but to be honest I am not ready for that stage in my life. When someone says, "Aubrie, if you are moving forward and on with your life then why are you not married?" The truth is that I am not ready to be married. Not yet. I still have things that I need to do before I move on to the next stage of my life. Moving forward to me is not necessarily moving on to a husband and kids. Instead I would like to move forward with my relationship with God and get my personal life squared away before I try to take on a marriage and a family.

I do like to date and go out with guys but for now I just want to have fun meeting new people and enjoying my friend's company. I have seen a lot of hurt in relationships and a lot of things not work out. I have actually been in relationships where it didn't work and for now I am happy being single and being able to do whatever I want, whenever. There is no rush to get married and have children. I want to enjoy dating and not rush into anything too fast.

I have never really had a lot of free time due to skiing and now that I have several books out my schedule is even more insane. I have book signings and interviews to go to, making dating and finding time for a guy difficult. One day I do want to be married and have children but now is not the right time. Sometimes I feel that there is not enough time in the day. 24 hours is all we get, really? Well I have to cram a lot in with the time that I do have and that can be challenging as well.

Some of the things I have to think about are, "With all of these books coming out and interviews that people want me to do will I have time to ski? Will I still be putting God first and have everything else come second? How busy will my life get? What is coming next in my life?" I often think about how many people will want to read my books and what it will be like to hear people talking about me and what I wrote. It was the strangest feeling when my first book came in and all of the sudden it hit. "I am an author."

It is awesome where life can take you. One day you wake up and things are the same and the next BAM! Things are different. You never know when God is going to want to use you or what he will want to use you for. God is full of surprises and you just never know when he will say, "Well, this is what I want you to do. Here it is." When that day comes it is so exciting but at the same time a little scary because your entire world will change, and for the better.

Your turn: I was only 15 when God decided to use me and show me what he wanted me to do with my life. God had something bad happen to me so he could use me to show others that when there is a will there is a way.

Write about a time when God gave you a gift. What was it that he gave you?

_____

_____

_____

_____

_____

_____

_____

_____

_____

_____

_____

_____

_____

_____

_____

_____

_____

_____

_____

_____

_____

_____

_____

_____

_____

_____

_____

_____

_____

_____

Your turn: Have you ever inspired someone? What did you do to inspire them?

Your turn: I am planning on going to Haiti on a mission trip to help kids who have lost their families and homes. I am going to build a new home for them and help give them food and a better life. I will probably play some sports and hopefully bring happiness in their lives.

If you could go anywhere in the world where would you go and why? What would you do?

_____

_____

_____

_____

_____

_____

_____

_____

_____

_____

_____

_____

_____

_____

_____

_____

_____

_____

_____

_____

_____

_____

_____

_____

Your turn: After the accidents I started to live every day like it is my last. It is important that I do not waste one minute in my life and that I do the best I can and always try my hardest with everything that I choose to do.

What are your beliefs about life? Are you the type of person that waits for life to be handed to you or do you get out and experience everything that life has to offer?

_____

_____

_____

_____

_____

_____

_____

_____

_____

_____

_____

_____

_____

_____

_____

_____

_____

_____

_____

_____

_____

_____

_____

_____

_____

Your turn: Write down every single thing that you want to do with your life. What do you want to accomplish before you die?

Your turn: Growing up I had everything. I was able to get new skis every year and one time I got two pairs in one season. My family put a lot of time and effort in my skiing and my success in the sport. I was not your typical teenager who was able to go out to parties and hang out with friends on the weekends. Every Friday after school and even during the weekdays my parents would take me up to the mountains and I would be in the gym or on the mountain training.

It was not that I wasn't allowed to hang out with my classmates after school. I chose to ski and be with my friends on the ski team instead of my friends at school. Growing up I was not into the party life, drinking, sex, drugs, etc . . . My focus was on school and sports. My parents had a rule that if I was to ski that my GPA had to be a 3.0 or higher. If it dropped I was not allowed to hit the slopes and do the things that I loved.

What rules do your parents have for you? What is growing up like for you?

_____

_____

_____

_____

_____

_____

_____

_____

_____

_____

_____

_____

_____

_____

_____

_____

_____

The first snow just fell and Aubrie is going to check it out

Aubrie and her mother, Claire, skiing in Durango CO

Summer time: Aubrie plays golf with
her mom in Breckenridge

Aubrie and her mother, Claire, in Vail for a fun afternoon. We wanted to change things up a bit so we decided to ski Vail, which was just beautiful and so much fun.

Christmas day: Aubrie and her family go skiing all day. It is a tradition in our family to ski on Christmas then go out to dinner and open presents after the mountain closes. We like to have relaxed and laid back holidays.

Aubrie in Hawaii doing her other favorite sport,
stand up paddle boarding and surfing.

Aubrie playing after a day of skiing. She is riding a snowskate, one of her other favorite winter sports. It is always difficult to get Aubrie to come inside to warm up.

She just likes to stay active.

Aubrie on a family hike. Aubrie and her dad like to climb 14,000 foot mountains in Colorado. This picture was taken next to Longs Peak, one of the more difficult climbes.

The day before this photo Aubrie climbed both Grays and Tory's, two 14,000 foot mountains in the same day.

Thank You

Thank you for reading my story. I hope that I have encouraged you to go for your dreams and work through any rough issues in your life. If you would like to see how I am doing and see any other books that are out or coming out please visit my website at www.aubriemindock.zoomshare.com or www.aubriemindock.com. I will have updates posted on my competitions and books.

I want to give a special thanks to my family who has been a huge support and so encouraging to me. I love you guys. Thank you for everything that you do for me. I am so blessed to have all of you in my life. I want to give a special thanks to my mom and dad for putting up with me while I figure things out with my life. Thank you for all of your love and support.

I would also like to thank the Breckenridge and Winter Park ski patrol for saving my life and being there for my family when they were concerned about whether or not I would pull through. Thank you for keeping the slopes safe.

Journals

Your turn: Did you know that the people you hang out with have a huge influence on your life. I remember having some really good friends growing up who were supportive and understanding. Today my friends are amazing. They are always happy for me and they want to support me and be there for me. I also want to support them and be there for them as well.

What are your friends like? Who do you hang out with? Why do you hang out with them? What kind of influence do they have in your life?

_____

_____

_____

_____

_____

_____

_____

_____

_____

_____

_____

_____

_____

_____

_____

_____

_____

_____

_____

_____

Your turn: Did you know that "Depression is one of the most common emotional ailments?" (Psalm 42:5,6) When I was in both of my accidents, especially after my second accident I became depressed. "What do you want me to do with my life now Lord?" I had no clue why something bad happened. "How am I supposed to use this for good?" I got over my depression by believing in God, that God would guide me and help me. I put all of my trust in God, that he would heal me and bring good into the bad.

What do you do when you become depressed? How do you handle depression?

Your turn: "People who are faithful to us accept us and love us, even when we are unlovable," (Psalm 40:10). How are you faithful to those around you? Why is it important to be faithful?

Your turn: "Life is short no matter how long we live. If we have something important we want to do, we must not put it off for a better day," (Psalm 39:4). If you only had six months to live, what would you do? How would you make the most out of the time you have left?

_____

_____

_____

_____

_____

_____

_____

_____

_____

_____

_____

_____

_____

_____

_____

_____

_____

_____

_____

_____

_____

_____

_____

_____

_____

_____

_____

_____

_____

_____

Your turn: "God wants to forgive sinners. Forgiveness has always been part of his loving nature," (Psalm 32:1,2). Is there someone in your life that you need to forgive? Who is this person and why do you need to forgive them?

Your turn: If you cheat your on small tasks during the day then you are cheating your way through life. Cheating your way through life is not a good way to live because you will never experience all of what life has to offer. Talk about a time when you cheated. It could be that you cheated on a test or in a sport. How did you feel after you cheated?

Your turn: Everyone has to face some kind of difficulty in their life time. I have faced many rough times but I realize that they are only bumps in the road. Today I realize that God is working through all of my difficult times and making everything positive and bringing good into my life.

How has God changed your life? How has he giving you strength?

Your turn: After my first accident I had to wait until Thanksgiving Day to ski again. The following Thanksgiving I was 16 years old. Getting back up on skis was the best day of my life. Not only did I ski again, I even raced. During Thanksgiving we focus on the blessings that God gives us. I believe that we should not wait until Thanksgiving to give thanks. We should be giving thanks every day to God.

What are you thankful for? Why are you thankful for these things?

Ski Bumps

Fact: Did you know that I lost part of my ear to frostbite when I was 17 years old? I was skiing in cold temperatures in Breckenridge and the wind went right through my helmet.

Fact: My mom Claire, started skiing when she was 19 years old. Today she is better than most of the women her age and she still skis the steep and deep.

Fact: Did you know that skiers have to wax the base of their skis? Waxing helps a skier go fast and keeps the snow from sticking on the bottom of the ski. Sometimes wax is not enough though. In extremely cold temperatures a ski can get a build-up of ice and a skier must take a scraper and knock the ice off.

Fact: Skiers have all kinds of waxes for their skis. There is wax for cold weather, warm weather and weather in between. There is special wax for racing and wax to fix bumps and scrapes in the ski.

Fact: Did you know that I have 5 pairs of skis? I have one pair for each event. Competitive skiers typically have several pairs of skis for competitions and even for certain conditions. I have race skis, powder skis, mogul skis, park skis and rock skis. Rock skis are used for early season and end of season conditions. They are skis that I do not care about.

Fact: In my family it is a tradition to ski on Thanksgiving and Christmas. We go out all day and ski, play outside after skiing then go out to dinner and celebrate our holiday later.

Fact: I learned how to ski in my back yard in Denver. When I was able to walk better on and off skis my mom took me to Loveland. When my brother was old enough to ski at the age of 1 my parents started taking us to Breckenridge.

Fact: My grandfather was in the 10th mountain division before becoming a park ranger in Rocky Mountain National Park. He is the reason all of us ski in my family.

Fact: Skiing is my favorite sport but I also love other sports such as surfing in Hawaii, stand up paddle boarding in Hawaii, swimming, other water sports, basketball, volleyball, tennis, ice skating, soccer and more. I would much rather play sports than watch them.

Fact: My brother, Austin, was a ski racer too. He decided to quit because he really enjoys skiing steep, deep powder. He was actually a better racer than me and had natural talent.

Fact: Austin and I were on Team Summit at Copper Mountain before joining Quantum Sports Club in Breckenridge.

Fact: After my second accident I had to take the rest of my college years off for racing. Giving up an Olympic dream was something that I was not going to do. Today I am back up and training. I was able to make a comeback.

Fact: I will never quit skiing. I will probably be 100 years old and still on skis.

Fact: My entire family loves skiing. I often ski with my uncles and cousins. When I am not with friends on the mountain you can find me with family.

Fact: Did you know that I like to teach skiing? I go to Breckenridge often and teach my friends to ski. One of my friends bought a pair of old skis and boots and she is giving skiing a go.

Fact: To this day I still get questions on why I got back up. People wonder how I could ever step into another binding after two accidents. I tell them that skiing is my passion and you cannot quit what you love.

Fact: People ask if I ever think about the accidents when I am skiing. My answer to that is yes. When I am having an off day and not skiing my best it is because I am usually thinking about what happened to me. I try not to let it affect me but sometimes those memories creep into my mind.

Fact: I often hear, "Do you ever feel pain from your accidents?" The answer is yes. Sometimes if it is really cold I will feel where I fractured my skull. Actually, it took about a year for my head to stop hurting in the area where I fractured it. My seizures went away after several months after my second accident. Today I am not too affected by it but sometimes I can feel a little pain.

Fact: I get asked a lot where I like to ski on the mountain. My favorite runs are the Imperial chair over on Peak 8 and Rocky Mtn. Peak 7 is also a blast. I tend to stay away from Peak 9 because there are typically a lot of people. Peak 10 is also fun. I like anything that is steep and where I can get some speed.

Fact: Breckenridge is my favorite place to ski because I love the town and I know the area well. Last season my mom and I took a trip to Vail and hit up some of the more difficult runs. We had so much fun and are planning on skiing more areas this season.

Fact: My mom will go down anything. She is not too big on the bumps but she loves the steeps.

Fact: Some of my favorite things to do when I am not skiing are going to movies, hanging out with friends, playing with my dogs, other sports and being with my family.

Fact: My family is pretty cool. I know that most people think their parents are just weird but I actually think my parents are great parents. Growing up they would let me skip school a lot but only as long as I kept my GPA at a 3.0. One time I wanted new skis and my dad made me get a 3.5 GPA before he would buy the twin tips for me.

Fact: After my second accident I really got into freestyle skiing. You can't get hurt in the air!

Fact: When I was only 12 years old I got about 30 feet of air off a run called Spruce. Spruce is a black that is under the Colorado Super Chair in Breckenridge.

Fact: On my phone I have an app that tells me how fast I am going on skis. I have clocked myself at speeds as fast as 70 mph.

Fact: My family owns a ski in, ski out place in Breckenridge. After a day of skiing you can usually find me on a snow skate playing on a trail behind my house.

Fact: Did you know that there are moose in Breckenridge? My mom and I were actually attacked by a bull moose August 2008. We were walking my dog Bailey and heading up to the Breckenridge Outdoor Rec Center when we came upon an angry moose on a trail. The animal charged, hit me then jumped over me and ran after my dog. My mom was able to get in the trees because she was behind me a ways and heard the commotion.

Fact: Breckenridge has a new Gondola. Did you know that dogs are allowed to ride it? I bring my puppy, Kai on it all of the time and she loves it.

Fact: If you are planning a trip to Breckenridge some fun activities are:

> Dog sledding
>
> Ice skating
>
> Go to the rec center in town and swim and climb the rock wall
>
> Shop (for shopping lovers only)
>
> Go to the cookie shop on Main Street
>
> Go to the Top of the World restaurant. If you don't eat there at least watch the sunset
>
> Go to the movies. There is a theater in Dillon.
>
> Snow Shoeing
>
> Ice fishing
>
> There is a gold mine adventure in Breckenridge

Fact: Did you know that skiing is easier to learn than snowboarding but more difficult to perfect? Snowboarding is the opposite, more difficult to learn but easier to perfect.

Fact: If you do not like long lift lines the higher up you go on the mountain the shorter the lines are, usually. It also depends on the season you are coming to Colorado. If it is in the middle of winter break you are going to be stuck in lines.

Fact: I do not like to ski the last two weeks of December because there are too many people in town. If I do ski it is on Christmas only.

Fact: I have traveled the country to ski.

Fact: I have taken many bad spills but usually I just get back up like it was nothing.

Ask Aubrie

Here are some common questions I get and my answers to them. Some people want to know how I survived and why I came back to skiing while others want to know what Heaven was like. Below you will read my answers to common questions asked.

Question: Aubrie do you think that the accidents had an impact on how you ski today?

Answer: Skiing has always been a part of my life. When you ski accidents do happen. Most of the time you fall and get back up like it was nothing. After my two accidents my skiing has not really changed. I am still the same skier, if not better and stronger than I was before the accidents. The accidents did not have an impact on my skiing ability but they did have an impact on my life. I believe that my life is actually better today because the accidents happened. I am able to reach out to more people than I ever was before it happened. When I ski I realize how lucky I am to have my sport back and today I teach others to ski because I do not want people to be afraid of the sport after they hear about what happened to me.

Question: What was Heaven really like?

Answer: There is no way to really describe Heaven. Heaven was perfect. There was pure happiness and joy. What really struck me was the light. It was like the sun in the way it lit up the sky but it was white and brighter than the sun. In Heaven there is no sun. There is light but it is all white, as white as snow.

Question: Did you see God in Heaven?
Answer: I did not see God in Heaven but I could feel him. God was all around but I did not actually see him. When I went to Heaven I saw my grandfather, PopPop.

Question: Were you afraid to get back up on skis after your second accident?
Answer: I was not afraid at all. There was no fear. I was actually stoked and couldn't wait to get back out. Skiing is my passion and without it I wouldn't know what to do.

Question: How much pain were you in after both of your accidents
Answer: There really was no pain during my accidents. During my first accident when I was 15 years old I kind of felt a "crunch, crunch" in my knee when I walked to ski patrol but there was no pain. During my second accident I did not really feel any pain at all. I was so out of it that I couldn't really focus on the pain. I just kind of kept going to sleep.

Question: What was recovery like?
Answer: Recovery was hard. It was extremely painful and tough. Recovering from any injury is painful but when you have numerous injuries that are healing getting better hurts a lot. I tried not to take pain medication though because I wanted to be aware of my surroundings and what was going on around me. I did not want to be all drugged up.

Question: How long did it take the ski patrol to get you off the mountain after your second accident?

Answer: I do not remember because I was in Heaven.

Question: What was the worst part about your accidents?

Answer: During my first accident it was tough knowing that my brother was watching me die. I didn't want him to think that I was in pain. I didn't want to leave him wondering how bad I was hurting. During my second accident it was tough because I had just hugged my mom and said, "I'll see you in a couple minutes," then it happened. It was tough knowing that I would be leaving my parents behind and that my mom would be left with that last hug goodbye. Leaving those I love most was tough. I was not concerned for myself because I knew that no matter what I would be okay. It was my family that I was sad for because I would be in Heaven and they would be left without me.

Question: Did dying scare you?

Answer: There was no fear. I was not afraid to die. Death is beautiful, not something to be afraid of. It is peaceful. Heaven is for real and it is the most beautiful thing you will ever see. There is no need to fear Heaven and what God has in store for us after we leave this earth.

Question: Did quitting ski racing ever cross your mind after your accidents?

Answer: No, never. I have always wanted to be a professional athlete and I was going to work hard and get back up no matter what. Skiing is in my blood and I will never quit this sport.

Question: When you had to get up and talk to groups after your accident did you find that difficult?

Answer: Yes, very challenging. The reason it was difficult to talk was because I stuttered. My head injury left me with a stutter that I had to overcome. The thing is once I started to talk all of my fears went away because people were very kind and understanding of the situation. They did not judge me or laugh at me when I would mess up. Everyone was sincere and really wanted to hear what I had to say. I am glad that I had the opportunity to reach out to so many people.

Question: Why do you teach skiing now? Doesn't it take time away from your training?

Answer: I teach skiing because I want to pass this sport on to others. I love watching people get the hang of skiing and see how happy they are after they accomplish a new sport. Teaching skiing does take away a lot of time from my training but that is okay. I still get tons of training in and I do enjoy going out with friends and just having fun.

Question: You say that you like to surf. Where is your favorite surfing spot?

Answer: The big island of Hawaii.

Question: How did you learn about God?

Answer: My parents. I would go to Sunday school and youth group growing up.

Question: What are the most important things in your life?

Answer: In order: God, family, friends, skiing, other sports

Question: How long is a typical ski season?

Answer: It depends on the snow but usually November through April. Sometimes I go to other places to ski during the summer months so for me it could be year round.

Question: You went back to school after your accident and decided to finish and tough it out. It could have been so easy for you to quit and drop out for the semester. What advice would you give to my daughter who is thinking about dropping out of high school?

Answer: In the United States we are so lucky to have the opportunity to go to school and get an education. In many countries women are not allowed to go to school. Education is so important and can lead to great things. It is important to stay in school and do your best because when you grow up you want to be able to read and write. You will want to get a good job and know what is going on in your world. I am so glad that I stayed in school and finished my degree. It could have been easy for me to say "I quit" and give up on school but I knew that I had to go back. I would say to your daughter to just enjoy high school and being young. There are so many great things this world has to offer and you will regret dropping out.

Question: Is snow skiing really that dangerous? Can't people make it safe so you do not get hurt like that?

Answer: Skiing, like any sport, is dangerous. People die every year on the mountain. There are things you can do to make the sport safer for you and your family. One thing to make skiing safer is to get an instructor. If you do not know how to ski or you need to improve your skills hire someone who knows the mountain and who can show you around. People get in trouble on the mountain when they get stuck on a run that is too difficult or they misread the signs. Some people think that skiing is easy and they can just jump on a pair of skis and just go. The truth is if you want to stay safe and have fun while you learn you need someone who is qualified to teach you. If you take precautions then you are less likely to go home with an injury.

Question: After your second accident did you know that you were dying?

Answer: No. I actually had no clue that I was dying. When I was in Heaven I knew that it was Heaven but the words death, dead and dying never came to mind. I knew that I was hurt bad but I didn't really feel pain or know that I was dying. I wasn't suffering like a lot of people think I was.

Question: What is it like to have your books published and have people talk about what happened to you?

Answer: I am stoked that I am an author because hopefully through my writings I can reach out to others and give them hope for their future. My goals through my books are to share God and help others overcome their fears. As for people constantly talking about what happened to me and bringing up the accidents it can get annoying. I do not like to focus on the accidents. Instead I would rather focus on seeing others learn to ski and enjoy the sport as much as I do. I want others to focus on reaching their goals and using my story to help them overcome whatever is in their way. I do not want to dwell on what happened to me. Instead I want to use my accidents and have them be the focus for hope and a future. I want others to see the good that came out of these events and not focus on the negative of the falls.

Question: You made it to Nationals after your second accident. What was that like?

Answer: I was so happy that my team made it to Nationals and actually couldn't control my excitement. I remember calling my parents and being like, "Mom, Dad, I made it to Nationals. Can I go with my team?" Soon everyone knew, and it was one of the best days in my life.

Question: When talking about the accidents what do you want people to know?

Answer: I want people to focus on the good that came out of my accidents. I want people to know that I have a great life now and that I will have a good successful life. I do not want to dwell on the fact that I almost lost my life twice. I want to focus on what the accidents brought into my life, which is a new appreciation for life.

Question: What are your future goals?

Answer: I still want to make the Olympics but this will be my last time trying because I want to reach out to others and show people that although bad things happen in life good will always come through. You never have to lose your dreams and give up on yourself. I want to show people that if you put your mind to something anything is possible.

Question: Do you snowboard too?

Answer: No. I only ski. I have snowboarded but I can do more tricks on skis so I stick with skiing.

Question: What are your favorite days to ski?

Answer: I typically only ski during the week. Weekends are just too busy. Sometimes I have to ski on the weekends because that is when my family and friends can ski. If I want to ski with them then I have to ski weekends but I try to just stick to skiing during the week.

Question: Do people recognize you a lot now that you have books published?

Answer: Yes. People will come up to me and say that they really like my books and ask questions about skiing and stuff.

Question: How often do you travel out of state for skiing?
Answer: The skiing is so good in Colorado that I do not really
           go anywhere else.

Question: What are your favorite runs in Breckenridge?
Answer: The steep ones! I like everything really but the steeper
           the better.

Question: How many days a season do you typically ski?
Answer: It depends on the snow and the conditions. Last year I
           skied every day but this year the snow is not as good so I
           have only been able to go out once and only for a couple
           runs.

Question: How often do you get new gear?
Answer: Well, every year I typically get something new. It is
           funny because most girls my age obsess on what to wear
           to a college class or on a date but I obsess on what to
           wear out on the mountain. I have a lot of coats and gear
           from all of my years skiing and it just keeps on coming.

Question: What is your favorite piece of equipment?
Answer: Well I recently got a new outfit for Christmas so I
           would have to say my new orange and pink coat. I also
           really like my new pants. They are pretty awesome. This
           season I also got a new pair of skis that are really fast and
           custom made boots. I am very lucky.

Question: Do you always wear a helmet when you ski?
Answer: Yes. I will never ski without one. When I teach my
           friends to ski I even make them wear one. You just never
           know.

Question: When you were in Durango what was your favorite mountain to ski?

Answer: In the Durango area it was Wolf Creek but I would take a lot of trips home to ski in Breckenridge and other surrounding areas. Nothing beats the summit county area for skiing.

Question: What was your favorite part about college?

Answer: Skiing of course. I remember one time my mom came to visit me and I decided to ditch classes with my roommate. We went skiing at Purgatory, which actually was not open yet because it was early season. My roommate and I couldn't wait any longer to ride though so we went up and hiked. My mom knew that I was skipping school but she didn't care because my grades were very good. She just laughed about it and let us go.

Question: As you look back on what happened to you would you ever take back time and not have gone skiing those days?

Answer: Nope. I would never want to change what happened to me because now I have the opportunity to inspire others and reach out more than I did before my accident occurred.

Question: What does your family think about you racing again?

Answer: They are fine with it really. I mean skiing is a huge part of our lives and it is something we all do as a family. They actually want me to race and be back on the slopes.

Question: After the second accident did you ever think that you would be able to inspire so many people?

Answer: I have a strong belief in God and I know that he has good come out of the bad. I knew that God would use my accidents for something good but no, I did not know that I would be able to inspire others after my accidents.

Question: Do you stay in touch with anyone from your college ski team?

Answer: I do not really stay in touch with anyone from the team because I was only on it for one season before having to quit and recover. However, I do stay in touch with people from my college and I am good friends with some of them still. I loved college. It was an awesome experience and I met some amazing people.

Question: When you were taking a break with ski racing did you think that your dreams of making the Olympics were over?

Answer: Yes I did. When I had to take 3 years off ski racing I thought that I would never get back up but not only did I prove others wrong, I proved myself wrong. I am back up and on the race course once again.

Question: If you could ski every day again this season would you?

Answer: No because I want to do other things besides skiing too. I like to snow skate and ice skate so sometimes I take days off the slopes to play other sports. Sometimes I just want to be in Denver with my friends and watch a movie or hang out. I do want to ski most days though. It is hard to take a lot of time off the mountain.

Question: Why did you never ask God why these accidents happened?

Answer: I am not one to feel sorry for myself. There were days when things were tough but the last thing I wanted to do was dwell on the fact that I was injured. I wanted to focus on the positive instead of the negative.

Question: Can you describe Heaven?

Answer: Heaven is beautiful and perfect. I remember seeing light when I was there. The light was white, like the snow but it surrounded me and my grandfather. It reminded me of sunlight but it was white instead.

Question: Most people would have quit school and recovered at home. Why did you go back to school?

Answer: I did not want to miss out on my second semester of my freshman year. I really wanted to get back to normal life as soon as possible.

Question: Was it difficult going back to school after your second accident?

Answer: It was so hard. More than anything I wanted to be with my family but I knew that if I was going to succeed that I needed to go back. I was in a lot of pain and going back was one of the most difficult decisions I've had to make.

Question: Why did you decide to get back up on skis so soon, before you were recovered?

Answer: Skiing has always been a part of my life and I really wanted to get back up. I love skiing and I couldn't even imagine not being on the mountain. It was just something that I had to do if I was going to be happy.

Question: What are your future goals?

Answer: I would like to inspire others to go for their dreams and to dream big. I want to reach out to kids and give them hope for a future. I hope that one day my story can help others succeed.

Question: What was the best thing that has happened to you since the accidents?

Answer: Being able to inspire others has been a great gift. I am so glad that I have the opportunity to help others go for their goals. I never thought that I would be able to use my story to help others.

Question: Do you think that you will make the Olympics?

Answer: I do not know. If I make them then I will be so happy and it will be my dream come true but if I do not make them then I'll be fine with that. Today I am focusing on giving others the gift of skiing so really making the Olympics, I don't know.

Question: Is Breckenridge still your favorite place to ski?

Answer: Yes, and it always will be.

Question: So, you and your mother were attacked by a moose? Do you want to talk about it?

Answer: Yes, my mother and I were attacked by a moose in Breckenridge while hiking under the Snowflake chair lift on our way to the BOEC lake. It is a long story that will have to be saved for another time.

Question: So, do you do all of the tuning of the gear in your family?

Answer: Yes I do. It was actually a chore growing up and to this day I still wax and sharpen the edges.

Question: Do you ever get annoyed by beginners on the mountain?

Answer: Well, I do but I try to be respectful. They are out for vacation and they want to try a new sport. Although beginners can be annoying they are just like the rest of us, out to have a good time. As a skier it is important to respect everyone, even those who are first timers.

Endnote

If you are struggling with anything or something is just too tough to deal with that is okay. Life is not always easy. There will always be ups and downs. All of us have struggles in life but that does not mean that we use our struggles as an excuse to be down all of the time. If you are having a difficult time coping with something I would suggest praying. Pray and ask God to show you how to use your bad for good. Ask him to help you turn your life around.

It is easy to fall into a depression when things just do not go your way. If you are having problems finding work, getting through school, doing well in sports or whatever you have going on in your life then maybe you just need to sit back and relax. Take some time off and rest your mind. Try to focus on something fun rather than all of that stuff that is stressing you out.

I hope that through my story you are able to find some hope for your future. Please do not give up on your goals or life if you are thrown a rough hand. God promises that good will come out of the bad. He uses our bad for good and I know that he will use you for something great. I hope that you find strength and courage through God and that your life is filled with many goals and dreams.